Lorna

Christmas 1946

ABOUT CONDUCTING

The empty space (24' x 8') in front of the Trumpets and Trombones, is to give the Trombone players plenty of room to work their slides, and to avoid the bells of these instruments being just behind the ears of the Horn players. Nothing is more trying than to play any musical instrument, with a Trumpet or Trombone blowing just a few inches behind your ear. Many sensitive amateurs have left an orchestra because of this. Therefore the largest and most spacious room should be secured for the weekly band rehearsals.

BASS DRUM   CYMBALS   TRIANGLE   SIDE DRUM   3

1st TRUMPET   2nd TRUMPET   3rd TRUMPET   4th TRUM

GANGWAY

2nd VIOLINS DESK XI
2nd VIOLINS DESK X
2nd VIOLINS DESK IX
2nd VIOLINS DESK VIII

1st HORN   2nd HORN   H

BASSOONS   1   2   BASS DOUBLE

GANGWAY

2nd VIOLINS DESK VI
2nd VIOLINS DESK V
2nd VIOLINS DESK IV
2nd VIOLINS DESK III
2nd VIOLINS DESK II
2nd VIOLINS DESK I

CLARINETS   1   2   CLAR BASS C

OBOES   1   2   OBO COR A

GANGWAY

1st VIOLINS DESK XII
1st VIOLINS DESK XI
1st VIOLINS DESK X

FLUTES   1   2   FLUT PICC

GANGWAY

1st VIOLINS DESK VI
1st VIOLINS DESK V
1st VIOLINS DESK IV
1st VIOLINS DESK IX
1st VIOLINS DESK VIII
1st VIOLINS DESK VII

VIOLAS DESK IV   VIOLA DESK V

VIOLAS DESK I

1st VIOLINS DESK III
1st VIOLINS DESK II
1st VIOLINS DESK I

Although six of each of the wood-wind band are set forth on this plan, with the gangway on the Conductor's left, the same plan should be adopted with only two or three each of the wood-wind, with the 1st players in line, one behind the other, 2nd players ditto—so that the conductor can, at a glance, see his 1st wind players, his 2nd wind players, his 3rd wind players. He must insist upon this radiating line form, from the Conductor's stand.

PLAN (a)

TEUR ORCHESTRA, ON THE
R LARGE SCHOOL ROOM)

CHAIRS

MUSIC STANDS

LENGTHENING PLY-WOOD BOARD
WITH A TWO INCH LIP (14" x 12")

FLOOR SPACE THAT TWO MU-
SICIANS OCCUPY, ENABLING THEM
TO BOW AND PLAY IN COMFORT

The lengthening board on the music stands,
for Flutes, Oboes, Clarinets, Bassoons, Horns,
Trumpets, etc., are generally only used by the
1st & 2nd players in the wood-wind department—It saves a stand, and often when the
1st & 2nd parts are written on two staves, the
single music stand for the 1st & 2nd players
is an advantage.

NI

TAMBOURINE & GONG

GLOCKENSPIEL & XYLOPHONE

CELESTA

1st 2nd 3rd
ROMBONE TROMBONE TROMBONE   BASS TUBA

4'

4th HORN   5th HORN   6th HORN

N BASSOONS   BASSOON

CLARINETS   CLARINET

OBOES   OBOE

FLUTES   FLUTE

VIOLAS DESK VI   VIOLAS DESK VII

LAS   VIOLAS DESK III

AND FORTE REQUIRED

CTOR

GANGWAY
GANGWAY
GANGWAY
GANGWAY
GANGWAY

DOUBLE BASSES
DOUBLE BASSES DESK VI
DOUBLE BASSES DESK V
DOUBLE BASSES DESK IV
DOUBLE BASSES DESK III
DOUBLE BASSES DESK II
DOUBLE BASSES DESK I

VIOLONCELLOS DESK XII
VIOLONCELLOS DESK XI
VIOLONCELLOS DESK X
VIOLONCELLOS DESK IX
VIOLONCELLOS DESK VIII
VIOLONCELLOS DESK VII
VIOLONCELLOS DESK VI
VIOLONCELLOS DESK V
VIOLONCELLOS DESK IV
VIOLONCELLOS DESK III
VIOLONCELLOS DESK II
VIOLONCELLOS DESK I

HARP

SIR HENRY WOOD
From a portrait (1936) by Flora Lion.

Sir Henry Wood

A B O U T

CONDUCTING

With a Prefatory Note by Hubert Foss

SYLVAN PRESS   LONDON   1945.

FIRST PUBLISHED IN 1945 AND REPRINTED BEFORE PUBLICATION
BY THE SYLVAN PRESS, 24-25, MUSEUM STREET, LONDON, W.C.1
AND PRINTED BY WILLIAM BROWN & CO. LTD., 11-12, BURY ST.,
LONDON, E.C.3.

MADE IN GREAT BRITAIN.

PREFATORY NOTE BY HUBERT FOSS

THE purposes of this book are clearly defined by its title : *About Conducting*. Earlier suggestions like "Advice About Conducting," were discarded after much thought as possibly giving a too generalised and therefore a wrong impression. For these pages do not discuss conducting in theory or conductors in person or orchestral works in analysis. The author in his opening sentences disclaims any intention, indeed asserts the impossibility, of writing a handbook, a primer, or a graduated course for conductors. Sir Henry Wood talks wisely about conducting—and no Englishman has ever lived better qualified to do so—to the young, and I venture to think his words will be treasured in store by the more experienced.

Wood was an inveterate note-taker. It was a life-time's habit. He would not rely on his memory for details, but quickly put them down on paper, so as to give his mind ample scope for contemplation of the larger aspects. On every possible occasion, on inconceivable pieces of paper of every size— folio note-books, backs of envelopes and letters, the laundry's stiffening cards, or whatever was handy— Wood would scribble at great speed and with an imperative urgency a thought that was passing through his head. It might be a detail of rough playing at rehearsal to watch over at the performance, it might be a philosophical truth about the nature of art—down it all went in that large, firm, virile hand, the very size of which would not allow his fingers to keep pace with his nimble brain. In these rough notes, there are words left out in the hurry of his expressive mind; the spelling is Elizabethan in its ready irregularities, sentences tail off as the meaning, already intelligible, needs a verb or a noun to complete its pattern. Many, it is obvious, will be repetitions of others, for Wood's fundamental views on conducting did not change, except to develop, in the course of years. Nor did his handwriting change greatly as he grew older, so that of two or even three notes expressing one thought in different words, it is difficult to tell from the evidence of the manuscript in what date order they come. Hundreds of these notes were kept in boxes and in the big folio duplicating books, and it is significant that in a letter to the writer Wood writes of " finding time to get together the material for the little book I want to talk to you about." He uses no more pretentious phrase than that. The material was there, the accumulation of a working, note-taking life of practical musicianship.

But this book was in no sense built or compiled out of these notes. It was deliberately written with the purpose of proving that the art of conducting cannot be taught by the written word. It was complete and ready for the printer before Wood died.

This instinct for recording details and points and ideas, for setting on record the true actuality of the moment, has a great importance in Henry Wood's life. It has been commented on adversely, as a barrier to spontaneity. In fact, it was the opposite : it was a means of ensuring a continuance of spontaneity, an aid towards the difficult task of recapturing " the first fine careless rapture." The greatest scholar was said by Ingram Bywater to be the man who knew where to look for his facts. Wood committed to tablets the minutiae, and knew where to look for the data on which to build his artistic conclusions. Yet he himself never felt any one interpretation of his own to be conclusive. When, just before he died, he was long engaged in re-studying Beethoven's Seventh Symphony, he said : " I always remember my last performance of a work." And, it should be added, he continually re-studied the most familiar scores—a point of advice made in these pages that many conductors will take to heart. The word " scholar," used a few lines above, has a special meaning in connection with Wood, therefore, for the reader will later observe that he demands scholarship of a conductor, but pleads that it may be practical scholarship, not academic.

The advice given in this book then is the practical advice from rehearsal and concert, not the theoretical advice from library or historical tradition. These pages are about to-day, " old saws and modern instances," and a great many modern saws here set down for the first time. One is reminded of W. H. Hudson's writing about birds. In Hudson there are none of the tabular classifications of the ornithologists. He was a field naturalist, making observations with his own eyes of patience. Henry Wood was an equal observer of men and women in the practice of music, and for want of a technical term, and to avoid coining a new jargon, we will call him the field naturalist of orchestral music. He is telling us of what he has seen, as Albrecht Dürer showed us how he himself formed his exquisite Roman alphabet. The craftsman admits us by means of this book into his studio, and talks to us of the secrets of his craft, of the right order and the proper sequence, of preparing the material, moulding it, and finally laying the patina on the perfected piece. It

is a privilege to hear him talk so intimately, so fear-
lessly of his methods. To learn quickly from this
advice is not easy, but I have no doubt of the
effect of Wood's words on the art and craft of
conducting, in time.

Not even when he is giving us shrewd hints on
copying parts, or clothes, or on the height of the
stand, does this craftsman ever let us forget his one
inspiring ideal—the proper rendering of the composer's music. The composer's watching presence
is felt in every chapter. It will be wished by many
readers that they could lay their hands upon a record
of Wood's application of his principles and his
genius to the works of the great masters. Those
who sang in choirs under his direction will remember
those remarkable books that he wrote (and printed
privately at his own expense) about the B Minor
Mass, the *Matthew Passion*, and many other works,
in which every detail of every man's and woman's
part, with phonetic spelling added, was detailed
down to the last mark of expression.

There was originally a plan to do something
of the kind. After tackling the first movement
of Beethoven's First Symphony, Wood abandoned
the idea. He realised that his means of com-
municating his musical genius to the public was
the baton, not the pen : he realised, too, that
words are a clumsy, inaccurate, and even tedious
medium for the expression of musical thought :
and, as he said to me, " It's been done by other
people." I agreed with this decision, though I
deplore our loss. Each man must take his music for
himself. If he can have the general guidance of such
a one as Henry Wood, he is lucky and can learn to
be wise and faithful in his generation.

The reducing of his continual and voluminous thoughts about conducting to an assimilable order was a task that occupied Henry Wood's close attention for many months. He wrote to me (we had seen the immense *Gentle Art of Singing* through the press together) as long ago as February, 1944, asking if he could see me to discuss the embryonic book. Engagements and other preoccupations prevented our meeting until after the interruption of the Jubilee Season of the Promenade Concerts. By that time the " Points " had been written and dictated—corrected and added to, and the remainder of the material, all of it in direct, conversational style. One could hear his inflexions as one read it. Here was no assumed literary manner ; this was a pen that spoke. One found some repetitions, some vivid oddities of spoken English that paper and print will not easily take, some hastily-said sentences that needed clarifying, even some *non-sequiturs*. Had he lived, all these little points would have been clarified and straightened out by Wood himself, and, further, he stated his intention of adding to it and expanding his thoughts in many places, once the Prom Season of 1944 was over.

A monument may be no less permanent because it is unpretentious. This little volume enshrines Henry Wood's daily practice as a craftsman ; it does not attempt to portray him as the artist he was. But here is wisdom to fit every circumstance of the conductor's round, and the rest—if we are each of us to learn to be a Henry Wood—the rest we must supply ourselves.

HUBERT FOSS

CONTENTS

INTRODUCTORY

" Will you write a book on conducting ? " " Will you give me lessons in conducting ? "

How often have I been asked those questions ! To the hundreds of such requests my reply has always been the same : the art of conducting cannot be taught by private tuition, diagrams, or the written word, and I am convinced that the art of conducting cannot be taught unless the student can face a complete orchestra, with an experienced conductor by his side *to watch every movement of the baton and gesture*, and to tell him why certain things do not come off. How the young beginner is to obtain this practical tuition and experience is a problem difficult to solve. The Royal Schools and other colleges offer instruction in the art of conducting, and I have no doubt occasionally find a student with a certain aptitude ; but there is a very serious, in fact an almost insurmountable, restriction, since a student conductor only gets a chance to direct the students' orchestra perhaps once a month (if that) in a movement from a symphony, or a short piece such as an overture. The orchestra should be available every week-day throughout the year for efficient instruction in conducting ; but how this is to be done is a problem I am unable to solve. Several quite promising young conductors from a students' class at the Royal Academy of Music have presented themselves to direct my Senior Students' Orchestra from time to time, and many, I am convinced, would have made good had an orchestra been available for very frequent practice in this art. But—and it is a very big *but*—even were this method made possible and an orchestra provided for daily instruction for every would-be conductor, I fear it would be quite valueless unless he is blessed with marked musical attributes.

The merely mechanical evolutions of beating time with the baton, as directed by time signatures, can be imparted through contactual instruction, but I most emphatically say that even this preliminary stick time-indication cannot be correctly taught through *written* instruction, because all diagrams of necessity indicate certain direct movements from one given point to another, and the *technique* of these evolutions still remains elusive. In fact the first thing to consider in this elementary time-beating is that *the baton is rarely still and rigid* as such diagrams must necessarily imply, because no diagram can satisfactorily describe the anticipatory upward lift before the beat, which is an essential in the art of direction.

Now, providing you have through private or class tuition mastered the elementary time-beating, there remains so much, and so many requirements that go to the making of a good *professional* conductor, that I think my best method will be to enumerate them under the following separate points, and treat each point more fully in short chapter form :—

THE POINTS

1. A Conductor must have a complete general knowledge of music.
2. He must have a *more than slight* acquaintance with every instrument of the orchestra, and if possible have had some intensive study of a stringed instrument, preferably the violin.
3. He must play the piano well.
4. He must have an impeccably sensitive ear, as well as rhythmic and interpretative sense.
5. He must be unafraid of the art of gesture.
6. He must be a perfect sight-reader and sound musician.
7. He must study the art of singing.
8. He must have a good physique, a good temper, and a strong sense of discipline.

MY EARLY START—A CAMEO FOR PARENTS

At a very early age my parents found that I was blessed with an artistic temperament. The artistic temperament does not necessarily mean all the things the real artist shuns—the Prima-donna-isms, unreliability, self-advertisement by any means to that end, disregard for ordinary customs, unfulfilled promises—in fact, insincerity of all sorts. Although neither of my parents was a professional musician, both were deeply interested in music and painting, and went out of their way to shape a course whereby my general education and my artistic education could develop side by side. I think that as quite a youngster I favoured painting rather than music; but music won, possibly through my early love for the organ. I was fortunate in my father's close association with St. Sepulchre's Church, Holborn, where he had been Principal Tenor for many years, and in this way I was allowed to practice on that beautiful Renatus Harris organ when my father's friend, the organist, was not giving lessons. My early association with this great organist, George Cooper, and his interest in my youthful aspirations, led to my being allowed to take services at St. Sepulchre's quite frequently when I was but twelve years old, and at the same period I acted as deputy organist at St. Mary Aldermanbury, while in 1883 I gave organ recitals at the Fisheries and Inventions Exhibitions.

Having made my choice in favour of music, my parents gave me every opportunity to follow my nose. I do not recommend parents to be quite so elastic as were mine, for I am certain that to-day a more general education is a great asset to a career in music, as to any other; for I find even after sixty years with my baton that I ought to be more alive to questions of finance, law of libel, copyright laws, and a hundred-and-one other problems where an early education in business methods would help. Not the least of these is the apparently clear and friendly phraseology of business letters to-day, which, after a while, you find need a lawyer's education to understand properly, so as to discover what was *not* said but what was really in fact the point. I would not recommend very young people to be up into the small hours of the morning, as I was so often taking part in my father's chamber-music evenings at home every Sunday and Monday; although these musical evenings gave me an insight into and a fairly general acquaintance with the indescribably lovely chamber-music repertoire. My father was an amateur 'cellist and singer but the other members of our party were experienced professional players, all eager to help this youngster, and they allowed me sometimes to play the first, sometimes the second violin, and the viola, when I was not at my appointed job at the piano.

I was not then old enough to enter the Royal Academy of Music, but I had daily lessons in the theory of music, counterpoint and harmony, the organ and piano; so that I was able to go to the R.A.M. as a fairly accomplished musician when I was fourteen, having meanwhile directed several amateur orchestral and choral societies, and held a paid post as organist at a church (St. John's, Fulham).

My parents were by no means well-endowed with spare cash, and all they had my father earned at his business as an optician and model engine builder; so that when I tell you, dear other children's parents, that mine sacrificed everything for my studies, you will see how alive they were to the fact that though but a youngster of immature years, I evinced undoubted evidence pointing to a future career, and how wisely they decided to give me every chance and the benefit of any doubt in forming that career. At the age of sixteen I had heard pretty well every great conductor of the time, for my father thought nothing of sending me to Berlin, Paris, and even Boston, U.S.A., including also the Bayreuth Festivals, armed with Cook's tickets and coupons, to attend possibly only one concert to see and learn from such men as Mottl, von Bülow, and Levi. Ah, parents! I can see your surprise when you consider a youngster of sixteen travelling as I did over Europe by himself; but you needn't wonder, for my parents treated me as a companion, just one of themselves—a wonderful trio—sending me forth on these journeys, bidding me learn, with their blessing and trust. " We trust you, Henry," they said. Of course this globe-trotting was planned for me most carefully—the hotels booked and just what money would be required for this and that, even to the tips, written down in my father's neat handwriting. How right was my father's advice and insight; his determination that I must not only hear and see every conductor possible, but that, since I had now determined upon my future career, I must endeavour to conduct *somewhere, something every day*—for fee or without! Experience was the thing! I took on anything, however good or bad the material. I composed and produced several comic operas, an oratorio, and many orchestral effusions, gaining experience every day until I undertook my first paid professional engagement as the conductor and musical director of a travelling opera company for the " untold wealth " of £2 a week! I can still see my mother's quick reckoning and her sweet smile as she said : " Well, it's not much, Henry, but your father will manage to make up what you will require."

From then on for a few years, Grand Opera was my hard way of experience ; frightful orchestras, which proved the very best training ; from September, 1889, with the Rousby Opera Company, on to assisting Sir Arthur Sullivan in his production of *Ivanhoe* (1891), Carl Rosa Company (1891), Georgina Burns and Crotty Opera Company (preparing for them an English version of *La Cenerentola*), until the first performance in England of Tchaikovsky's opera *Eugéne Onegin* at the Olympic Theatre, London. In this way I learned on the hard road of bad orchestras—travelling orchestras—bad and good singers, the *art of conducting*, by which I mean finding the means through beat and gesture to make those under my direction sing and play better than they really could. No one knows how invaluable these poor travelling companions are to the would-be *good* conductor, for he soon learns that the thing he wants does not come off, and sets about finding out the "whys" and ways to bring it off. It cannot be too much to say that no kind of income can be expected until such experience is at your command.

During my early years I had studied the various instruments of the orchestra, and could play passages pretty fluently on many of them—an accomplishment that was to guide me faithfully all my life in deciding the tempi of a work ; for of course the wind players cannot articulate at the facile speed of the violins, and such wind passages must frequently determine the tempo of a movement or work. How often these days does one hear the deplorable results of this want of knowledge of the instruments of the orchestra. I have been amazed at the lack of knowledge of the score evinced by solo pianists recently, taking passages with facile familiarity at a breakneck speed, through never having taken the trouble to study the full score of the concerto. If they had they would have found certain passages in the wood-wind or brass, every note of which requires " tongueing," and the only way the players could meet the situation was to slur the notes—at complete variance with the composer's directions. I suggest that all solo artists make a study of the full score of a concerto and get some practical advice regarding the speed at which certain instruments of the orchestra can articulate clearly, in the manner and tempi dictated by the composer.

I was perhaps very lucky in my youth to have heard *every week of my life* the great singers of the past—the fine vocal period (1880 to 1925)—accompanying most of them, and hearing them talk of their past experiences, the methods of their teachers, their sorrows and their joys. Further, I had lessons in singing from everybody who taught the art : Fred Walker, Gustav Garcia, Randegger, Fiori, W. H. Cummings, Duvivier, Edwin Holland, and old Manuel Garcia. I became the latter's accompanist (piano), and in this way I gained a working acquaintance with all the operas, concert arias, and oratorios, and learned the difficult art of accompaniment in this great school. In this way, too, I also took up the teaching of singing, often giving as many as fifty lessons a week in addition to my conducting and church appointments.

I am always thankful that my parents lived to see me on the high road which their undivided interests and sacrifices had made possible, for they both saw me start out in the year 1895 on the now famous "Queen's Hall Promenade Concerts," known to-day as the "Henry Wood Promenade Concerts."

MY POINTS FOR THE WOULD-BE CONDUCTOR.

Point I.—A Conductor must have a Complete General Knowledge of Music.

Such education as is to be obtained at the Royal Academy of Music, the Royal College of Music, in fact at all recognised schools of music, is absolutely essential right from the very beginning; harmony, counterpoint, orchestration, and so on.

If you have decided to make your career as a conductor it is of paramount importance that you study orchestration

Though you have no gift for composition, never mind, just peg away at scoring piano pieces, songs, etc., and so make yourself familar with the *perspective* of a full score. In this way you learn to see at a glance whether a work you may later on be called upon to direct is written correctly for the compass of the various instruments ; and familiarise yourself with the placing of the various instruments in the score. One hint: never make your full score on that out-sized manuscript paper ; firstly, it won't go into any suitcase or music-case, and you cannot conveniently carry it under your arm, and worst of all it won't stand on an ordinary pianoforte desk, nor is it safe on the ordinary conductor's stand. It wobbles and topples about, and makes the perspective of the score at an ordinary distance completely impossible ; instead of being able to see the whole lay-out of the score at a glance, your head has to travel up and down the page like that of a mario-nette ! I always maintain there is only one way to read such scores—they should be put on the floor at the foot of the rostrum if a *reading* perspective is to be obtained ! It is quite a simple matter to write for two instruments of the same name on one stave ; even in the percussion, one stave is adequate for two instruments. Eight percussion parts can be written quite clearly on four staves. Prokoviev writes for eight horns on one stave, making the reading of the score much simpler, and of course condensing the size of the paper.

This study of orchestration is of the greatest value to you later on when looking over a new work in manuscript, or even the printed edition, as it will assist you in readily spotting " niggers," and so save you many vexatious moments when you come to rehearse the work with an orchestra.

I don't like the method some composers adopt of treating certain wind instruments as *non*-transposing instruments ; it often leads to unnecessary confusion.

Learn to make your manuscript in a firm, clear, legible handwriting.

While you proceed with your studies at your Academy, College, or School, take every opportunity of attending concerts, opera, theatre, ballet, vocal or other recitals, and never miss the Students' Orchestral Rehearsals at your School of Music. Concentrate on hearing every concert and rehearsal possible, and ask permission of managements and conductors to allow you to attend orchestral rehearsals. You will readily obtain permission as a serious student from a recognised school, and if you have the pluck to do it, ask the conductor to allow you to sit on the platform at the back of the orchestra, from which angle you can learn so much. If you have now decided to take up the baton as a career, go and watch every conductor possible with your miniature score, it will guide you in a thousand ways in what *not to do,* perhaps much more than just what *to do.* Learn to watch the conductor's gesture and decide whether he has invited the result he gets ; once seen, a false gesture is never forgotten when later on you come to direct an orchestra yourself.

Point II.—The Conductor must have more than a slight acquaintance with every instrument of the orchestra, and if possible, some intensive study of a stringed instrument— preferably the violin.

Learn to play passages on every instrument of the orchestra, for in this way you will be able to judge the tempi of your passages for wind instruments and strings. Some instruments cannot articulate at the same speed as a violin. It is most helpful if you can play the violin pretty well and have studied with an acknowledged executant, as this familiarity helps you to decide your bowing and the marking of orchestral parts.

With the other instruments it is of invaluable assistance to you, too, in becoming familiar with the quality of tone each instrument *can* give at the hands of an accomplished executant, but *does* give in the hands of the beginner and of that hard-boiled player with no soul—the kind of player one meets, thank goodness, infrequently—who blasts forth oblivious of any finesse or tone colour, raucous and raspy ! Goodness knows I should know, for even my devoted parents were obliged to send me to a top back room when making my way with such instruments as the bassoon, horn, trumpet, clarinet, and so on.

In this way you learn from practical experience how just too devastating a " brassy " horn can be, but how velvety and mellow it should, and does, sound, especially these days when we are blessed with an unbeatable tradition in this department of the orchestra.   Can anything be more vulgar than the blatant shriek of a clarinet in its upper register ? Yet in the hands of an artist (and we have two or three in England) how lovely and liquid the tone is, and so beautiful in the middle harmony of an orchestra ! So likewise with the oboe, flute, and bassoon.   You must, in fact, train your ear to appreciate the real qualities of tone as apart from the mere facility of the player.

I always find an orchestral player either approaches a solo passage with a slap-dash, don't-care, go-through-with-it attitude, or (as I like to see it) with care and perhaps a certain nervousness.   In either instance endeavour, when first running through, not to *notice* this player. Go through it again and if you find the passage still "sticks," or is blatant, fluffy, or pointless, just remind him : "Take your own time, my friend, I am here to accompany you ; play it as the artist you are."   In this way it pretty nearly always comes off.

So, if your ear and training are what they should be to fit you for your job, you will so often be able to persuade your player to meet his solo passages with more confidence, and to cajole him into a more refined quality of tone and a better rendering. It is such a help, I do assure you, my friend.

The tone quality in all departments of the modern orchestra has changed even within my living memory. I can still hear the Crystal Palace Orchestra under August Manns, and the Richter Orchestra at St. James's, so hard and blasting, so different from the B.B.C. Symphony Orchestra and our other fine permanent orchestras of to-day. I have noticed so many piano students have no idea of the quality, power, and character of the modern wood-wind instruments. Even in Schumann's Piano Concerto, many is the time I have had to tell them to listen : " You are accompanying only one flute and it is playing in its lower register—it is not a trombone or a trumpet ! " I think it would be so helpful if students at our music schools were compelled to hear monthly recitals of an hour of the wood-wind, and other instruments of the orchestra, given by various professors of these instruments, with only a piano accompaniment, for in this way students would memorise and know the quality, power, and technique of the various instruments. It might help to curb some of these " speed " fiends too !

Point III.—The Conductor must play the piano well.

I must say emphatically it is essential for a conductor to play the piano really well. You will have to meet the instrumental artist, the singer, the chorus in preliminary rehearsal before meeting them with the orchestra, and if you can accompany fluently you come to the rostrum in no doubt as to what is to be done. This is not only satisfactory in concerto, aria, and choral work, but saves that precious and elusive master—time—during the orchestral rehearsal. It is essential in the study of a new work ; not only for timing, but it assists you in becoming familiar with the work.

I have always made it a necessity that all artists go through their work with me, preferably the day before a performance, and if you can accompany an aria or instrumental concerto, you will find that you " feel " the artist's interpretation, and he, your orchestral accompaniment. In my young days, when I was touring with a concert party as accompanist, a well-known impresario said of me : " Wood can never keep it up for the whole tour, he plays like an orchestra!" Well, you can accomplish much in this way if you can play really well. Your orchestral accompaniment can ruin the greatest aria sung by a great artist, and this is why I find it all important for a conductor to be able to accompany on the piano really well : he knows then how to accompany through the orchestra.

Another thing in which I have found the liveliest satisfaction —the help you can give to young artists. Your piano rehearsal gives them confidence, and you go to the rostrum knowing just where there is likely to be a groggy moment, and you can pull this young artist through an ordeal which, when once over, may be the prelude to a successful career.

The study of piano-playing is, I regret to think, usually approached with a view to becoming a solo artist, and I could wish our schools of music paid more attention to the art of accompaniment, for we find so few really good accompanists.

When you come to direct a choral work, your ability to accompany really well will assist you, and enable you to play the work yourself for the preliminary rehearsal and give your choir, accompanist, and choir-master an insight from the very start as to your requirements. How bad are some accompanists provided by choral societies ! It is just past my understanding. To play the piano really well and to accompany with sympathy are an absolute necessity, I assure you.

Point IV.—The Conductor must have an impeccably sensitive ear, as well as rhythmic and interpretative sense.

As quite a small boy I was able to name a note to a rap on the table, a knock on the door, the tinkle of a glass or cup. In fact, my father used to amuse himself by suddenly tapping anything at hand: "What note is that, Henry?" And my answer was verified on the piano. Luckily I was not often out by even the fraction of a semitone. This family fun turned out to be of lasting value in my work with the orchestra and singers.

Your first duty as a conductor is to make it imperative that every player tunes to the fork prior to your rehearsal and concert. I am amazed and shocked to note how often one has to listen to the opening work of a programme quite dreadfully out of tune ; and I say without hesitation that it is the conductor's fault. Conductors nowadays seem less and less fidgety about *intonation* : possibly because they are afraid of suggesting that the players tune in advance of a rehearsal or concert. But never mind the reason, the result is horrible and amazing to those listening to the first item.

I regret to say that the professional orchestral string-player rather resents your request that he should tune. He prefers you to remember that he is an accomplished artist able to adjust his fingers on the board of a violin, 'cello, etc. Yes, quite so ! But you wait until he is *obliged* in certain passages to use the *open* string ! In the early days of my Queen's Hall Orchestra I had a tuning machine built consisting of a silver harmonium reed, blown by a bellows and small wind chest. I insisted on every player filing past to tune before he went on to the platform. It was magical. Never did we hear some of the nerve-shattering " arguments " in unison passages, or between the strings and wind departments, like those we regrettably hear to-day. I still tune my Royal Academy Orchestra in this way ; go to their concerts and hear them for yourself, and you will come to the conclusion that it is worth the time spent on it. I can never reconcile myself to these academic musicians who can sit and glow with pride during the performance of a school orchestra quite out of tune. What is the first sense a musician should have in particular ?—ear, a sense of pitch and tone quality.

Tone ! Ah, here is where your study of the instruments of the orchestra trains your ear to distinguish good from bad tone quality, and this attribute is an essential factor in marking up or down certain instruments in certain halls.

The question of acoustics is a subject that I regret is so neglected in England. Think of it, an enterprising city, with a fine music tradition, decided to spend £350,000 or so on a hall, and set about it only to find eventually that although it is excellent as a medium for civic speeches, it is unsuitable, acoustically and architecturally, for the presentation of orchestral music. I can never understand why local authorities and architects give so little thought to the requirements for seating of a symphony orchestra and choir when constructing a hall for general purposes, such as are most Town and County Halls. It never seems to enter their heads that the presentation of symphonic music requires, firstly, special platform construction, and secondly, scientific treatment in such things as wall surfaces, carpeting, etc., if the hall is to be acoustically correct for an orchestra and chorus ; and it is pretty safe to say that if acoustically perfect for orchestral music, it will be an equally good medium for speeches and meetings. As you will be aware, the concert halls and various buildings in which we are obliged to make music in this country vary in size and structural substance. Here again is where your ear and musical sense and teaching will guide you to better representation of the music on hand in acoustically bad halls ; for with these conditions we have to be content until such time as every city follows the Government's lead, and recognises that serious music is an essential part of the social and educational system of 1944 and onwards, and realises also that an orchestra requires specialised architecture. Authorities must in time, and soon I hope, admit the value of serious music, and impose a small local rate with which to provide citizens with a means of healthful uplifting social entertainment at no greater cost than that vast Art Gallery which few visit.

All this brings me back to a " sensitive ear " ; if you have it, it will guide you in " placing " your chorus and orchestra to obtain the best results, say in a hall with dead dull acoustic properties ; while on the other hand certain halls require much modulation in the use of your brass, drums, etc., as the echo and reverberation from such departments in a small hall against a hard background completely obliterate all string tone. So here your " sensitive ear " advises you that all such departments in this hall must be marked down from *f* to *p*, and so on. You will be able to decide whether the back wall of the platform is going to make your brass and timpani too reverberant, or as the case may be, too muffled ; you will so request your players to modulate the *f*, or accentuate it. This applies, too, invariably to the basses, they are usually too inaudible. So do keep an ear and eye on this problem of architectural variance, especially in these days when orchestral performances so often take place in a theatre—for lack of real concert halls—where flies and back-cloth put *paid* to anything like the tone quality and volume of a symphony orchestra.

I have so often noticed that conductors do not *listen* to the orchestra when directing ; they are so absorbed in the act of conducting, score-reading, or memorising, that they forget to listen with critical ear. Here again I do insist that the preparation and study of the work on hand is the factor that will give you the much-to-be-desired faculty for critical listening.

Rhythmic sense!   By this I do not mean metronomic precision—this is essential of course during early studies—but a sense of rhythm that admits all you desire in freedom of interpretation ; yet the music hangs together in logical expression, as your individual musical taste dictates. All rubato and expression must remain within the main tempo, and must not spoil the flow of the rhythm One hears it often said : " Let the music speak for itself." Does it ? And if and when it does, what is the answer ?—dull, dead notes, just notes ! The great artists know how to apply a subtle tempo rubato and yet keep to the time within the bar : they truly borrow and pay back. How simple it is to direct such artists! Do you think I should have ever gathered together the great company of music lovers the Promenade Concerts have created, had I not taken full advantage of the whole gamut of human emotions which music can, and does, so adequately express, and is I maintain *intended* to express? Did I " let the music speak for itself " when I introduced the immortal Brandenburg Concertos to England at the Promenade Concerts ? No ! and if I had I am certain the man in the street would not have listened, and would not have come to fill Queen's Hall to overflowing every Bach night.

Music is a lifeless thing written down ; it requires interpretation to give it life. Indeed I have no patience with these people who quote loud and oft " let the music speak for itself." You will usually find such men are either completely unable to impose their own interpretation by means of will and gesture upon an orchestra, and so just let the *orchestra speak for itself*. The players will play all the notes and will possibly keep a more or less nodding acquaintance with the gentleman on the rostrum, but although that piece of writing has been given life, it is such a profoundly meaningless birth that it dies of its own utter inanity ! That great virtuoso conductor, Arthur Nikisch, once said to me when I told him how some people criticised my use of rubato, " My dear Wood, music is a dead thing without *interpretation* : we all *feel* things differently. A metronome can keep a four-square indication if they like it that way, but never forget that you should make every performance a grand improvisation even though you direct the same work every day of the year ! " Richard Strauss held, and still holds, I am sure, the same views regarding the interpretative artist. " Do what you like," he said, " but never be dull."

In my young days I heard really musical people say " Bach is just a sewing machine," and so I set about reading all I could lay hands on regarding his life and his voluminous output. I found that when I played Bach to a metronome, it was undoubtedly mechanical ; but having studied Bach's life, I knew that he was of an emotional character in which no mechanical routine could have existed, and I came to the only logical conclusion that he played and jotted down his thoughts as they came, and as with manuscripts of that period, added no expression or other marks. All expression was obviously self-imposed expression when seated at his organ, his clavichord or harpiscord. I am sure he varied his expression in any given piece according to his mood, for no man was ever a greater experimenter than Bach himself. Can you tell me that a man such as he, the father of twenty-one children, with many hundreds of compositions to his credit, always picking quarrels with the managements for having too few strings in his orchestra, a modern of the moderns of his time, was a man who merely jotted down notes on paper to be played as a " sewing machine ? " Never ! The difference between a modern concert performance before a large audience in a large hall and an *historical* performance in a small hall with instruments all constructed as in Bach's time, is a problem I have solved to my satisfaction, and to that of a vast concourse of Bach lovers.

Perhaps no composer left his scores so marked as did Elgar ; and yet how different the readings we hear these days, which goes to prove that however definitely marked a score may be, it can never be precise in every detail. No code of signs has proved adequate to lay down exactly what the composer had in mind. He can only hope that his tempi and expression marks are sufficient guide to control that person who prefers " the music to speak for itself," or again to control that speed fiend of the present day (alas !) who has only one idea, and that is to " brighten " things up. I have quite recently heard Tchaikovsky's Fifth Symphony so " brightened up " that certain passages were impossible to articulate even in the violin department, whose only hope was to slur them : and what on earth do you think the wood-wind and brass could do if the strings found the speed impossible ?

I have never " saved " myself—by this I mean reserved my energy ; but I am convinced that because my energies have been directed through legitimate means to an end, I have never wasted energy on fruitless experiments. I have heard performances only recently which have made me wonder, have we made strides as far reaching as I had hoped ? I have listened to a work such as *Benvenuto Cellini*, with all the stops out all the time, brass and drums blaring and thumping away, and no attempt on the part of the conductor to reason whether modification would not be desirable in such and such hall. Of course these days of broadcasting have much to answer for, since the technique of the controls' engineer can to a large extent produce just what *he* wants to hear, and not what is actually being picked up. I know quite well that in Sibelius's great Symphony, No. 1 in E minor, all the colossal crescendos and smashing climaxes are some-times whittled down and come over the air with but half the grandeur of tone quality heard in the Queen's Hall from which it is possibly broadcast; but even though you are aware of this levelling down of your interpretation, never allow yourself to remember anything but your audience in the hall, who pay for their tickets for the direct performance. A studio broadcast is of course a different matter.

Point V.—The Conductor must be unafraid of the art of gesture.

We are a shy people, timorous and afraid of what we call an " exhibition of temperament," and yet I assert that no conductor excels unless he is gifted with the physical ability to impose a literal translation of temperament through his gestures, of his interpretative sense and will. I even doubt that it can be perfected by close study for it is so much a matter of temperament, although of course it might be followed up, for instructive reference, by carefully *watching* every conductor possible, while comparing the score with his results. A conductor asks for what he gets from a professional orchestra, and if you follow his baton and left-hand gesture (I always say I paint the picture with my baton), you will note the answer and form your conclusions. If you were having an argument with some one who had not given you correct change, you would first of all put out your hand palm upwards and ask for more ; and if he argued, you would surely extend your hand still further in a gesture asking for yet more. A simple example, but one even the youngest of my readers can understand. Go and watch, too, the fine actor or actress of the stage and screen ; for after all music depicts the story, although in the more subtle and elusive medium of the unwritten word, and because it *is* a story which is left for individual interpretation, your gesture must be all the more definite and unmistakable if you are going to get it out of your orchestra. Go and watch every ballet ; I can suggest no better medium for the study of the art of gesture, for what a part the hands and arms play in ballet !

Mind you, there is no room for the conductor who throws himself about the rostrum, or uses his left hand to no purpose. Beware of vague and useless gesticulation with the left hand ; yet every gesture that receives the right answer from an orchestra is legitimate. I need not stress the point that your gestures should be carefully analysed always ; watch that left hand and ask yourself : " what do I mean to convey to my players ? Is it a graceful gesture ? Is that hand stiff and repressing, or is it delicately poised asking for light and shade, or indicating a player's entrance ? " All left-hand work must be carefully watched, and certainly not used as if the hand were the fin of a seal flapping about. A word of warning ! Whatever you do, don't take lessons in " conducting deportment," for unless your gesture is the spontaneous and natural outcome of your personal interpretative sense, it gets you nowhere with your ochestra, and merely looks awkward, self-conscious, and unnatural to your audience. it must be remembered that although the left hand is so important, every real request comes from the baton, and this is why I say most definitely that the art of conducting cannot be taught through the written word, for although you may master the purely technical gyrations of beating time it is the use of the stick-hand and the point of the stick which interprets the meaning of your requests.

The outstanding point is, don't be afraid to try to impart your innermost feelings through gesture. That reserve associated with us is a much-to-be-desired virtue in every work-a-day life, but musical thought is just that which takes us to realms and places not so near this earth, and so worthy of finding a means whereby we can spread this glorious message through lovely sounds—things not of the office, the shop, the factory, the coal mine, wherein those who work come to you to be refreshed in healthful recreation; and so your gesture will, or will not, be the means of imparting this message to an audience of potential music-lovers. If your interpretation is dull and dry, either through your inability to play upon your orchestra through your baton, or because you foster the let-the-music-speak-for-itself academics, you will possibly send some of your audience away unsatisfied, unrefreshed, and mystified since they had come to hear serious music for the first time. That is why I say " potential " music-lovers, for I am quite sure we can make everyone friendly with serious music so long as we make the presentation of it a profound oration through lovely sounds. In attaining this, gesture plays a tremendous part; all the nuance, all the story is in your hands (literally) to express.

Don't confuse my meaning. I distinctly adjure you *never, never, never* make a gesture that has no legitimate intention, instruction, or request behind it. Learn to approach a public performance with just the same concentrated detachment as that with which you take your rehearsal; you must never be conscious of an audience.

Point VI.—The Conductor must be a perfect sight-reader and sound musician.

I cannot speak too strongly on the absolute necessity of making yourself quite accomplished in this study before you take your stand facing a professional orchestra. Of course if you are one of the youngsters training through errors via the amateur orchestral and choral societies (as I did), you will have achieved ability in sight-reading, and this in no uncertain manner. If you are meeting an orchestra of professional players, you must remember that they are all first-class musicians and will spot with the utmost delight any rift in your armour of general knowledge of music and musical sense. A conductor is so often called upon by a player during rehearsal to decide a point, maybe a supposed printer's or copyist's error, an accidental ♯ instead of a ♭, or a wrong note; " we've got a third crotchet in such-and-such a bar," and so on. An outstanding case arose during the 1914-18 War, when Delius came to us and I produced his *Eventyr* at a Queen's Hall Symphony Concert. There occurred a debatable wood-wind chord, and turning to the composer by my side, I asked him if the note on the chord in the second beat was a G ♯ or G ♮ Delius's reply was : " I don't know, I'll leave it to you." Well, if a conductor had not command of the all-round musicianship I maintain is absolutely essential, he would have found himself at a great disadvantage, and in this specific case both the composer and players would have discovered the rift in his armour.

It is not beyond the orchestral musician to have his little joke or " dig " at the expense of a conductor in whom they " sense " the amateur approach, and to ask a question the answer to which every man in the orchestra knows. It is merely in the hope of catching you out. On several occasions I have attended rehearsals with a conductor in charge new to the game, or a man satisfied with his accomplishments, and have known that many passages in wind and brass departments have either been left out, or wrong notes have been played; and what a joke the players had behind their desks at his expense. I know of course that scores are studied prior to rehearsal, but it often happens that you are called upon to alter an item in the programme at the last moment, and so on, and have to read a fresh score at sight.

You must remember that I am advising you as to the best means of becoming a professional orchestral conductor, and that my warnings regarding the methods adopted by professional orchestras are proffered in that spirit; for the real professional orchestral musician I have nothing but unstinted praise to offer, and among them I count the friends of my life. I can assure you the professional player is ever waiting to give loyal support when he finds real talent on the rostrum, but for the ambitious amateur-cum-professional he has little sympathy, and will do his best to make him not only pay, but work his passage too!

We suffer much these days from the amateur with a safe income, whose activities do much to retard progress and stifle inspiration and enthusiasm, especially among the orchestral players. There is no other profession which presents an opening for the amateur like that of music. We don't go to an amateur dentist, or engage the services of an amateur doctor, because we feel beforehand all we would suffer at their hands; but with music, although actual physical suffering does not result from an afternoon or evening's music with amateur-cum-professional players and director, we come away unrefreshed and disinclined to repeat the dose.

Point VII.—The Conductor must study the art of singing.

Whether you have a voice or not does not matter. If you have a true so-called " conductor's voice " it is certainly an advantage; nothing is more fatiguing or irritating when, after some big fortissimo chords, the conductor stops and makes a request, and *not one word of what he wants* carries over the orchestra, and you find the percussion players straining, hands to ears, to catch his words. A voice which has no edge or *timbre* in it makes rehearsals very dull and very fatiguing. Old Garcia always teased me about my voice and said it would go through a brick wall, and told me never to sing in public. I promised him I never would but it has proved a useful conductor's voice, all the same thank goodness.

Anyhow you will have some kind of a voice ; all the better of course if it is of a good singing quality that carries. But it is neither here nor there, for our business is to study this branch of music as being another requirement which goes to the making of a good conductor in many and various ways. In learning to sing you will find that the first essential is breath control—the art of phrasing and taking breath at correct places. This first essential to singing is of inestimable worth in building up the purely physical requirement in the exacting demands imposed in the routine of a conductor. It develops abdominal muscular control and, if taught correctly, diaphragm muscles develop in support of this deep upward breathing and no conductor is worth a jot, or has any staying power, without this diaphragmatic control. Phrasing comes easily in the art of song, as the words guide you at the same time as the natural sense of the music, and this first-hand knowledge of singing assists you when directing wind instruments of the orchestra, for they, like singers, have to phrase and breathe. If the conductor is alive to this purely physical necessity, he can help his players to breathe together and so obtain perfect ensemble. Of course these " breath gaps " should be indicated by the stick, for although phrase marks should have received your attention when marking and bowing your parts, you can, by a certain little upward stick-gesture, control the breath intake of each player simultaneously so that they articulate together. *This is of the utmost importance.*

A word of advice—having studied the art of singing yourself, you will have learned that the human voice is a much more difficult instrument to play upon than any instrument of the orchestra, as it is subject to many outside influences, and that those little vocal cords are darned difficult to control! This you must always bear in mind when directing vocal stuff. Don't upset a vocalist's " reading " of a part in a choral work, or alter his conception of an aria, at the eleventh hour (I mean if there is only the one rehearsal on the day of performance), as the singer will have been preparing the work perhaps for months in his own particular style. It is quite unfair for a conductor to endeavour to dictate his reading, unless of course he sees to it that he has several rehearsals, or one piano rehearsal sufficiently ahead of the day of performance to give the artist time to adjust the unaccustomed reading into his or her voice.

The conductor is usually consulted regarding the casting of a choral work he is to direct, and here again knowledge of singing should guide you in making a choice of artists best suited for the parts they will be called upon to sustain. You will not invite a soprano with that distressing vibrato, with which, alas, we are only too familiar today, or the " hooty " contralto, whose tone colour blends ill with other voices, or the tight throaty tenor, who thinks only of his top A, or the doleful, gloomy bass-baritone, always flat in position if not in pitch. If every conductor refused to direct a work or aria with a singer so afflicted, we should soon raise the standard of singing, and the public would again find pleasure in this most beautiful department of music. Your knowledge of singing will enable you to choose a well-balanced quartet of singers, both in voice and style. It is a grave error to engage, say, a great operatic singer and fill in other parts with the truly lyrical or oratorio vocalist ; better a quartet of less famous artists whose style and timbre of voice blend. You may have in some artists fine Handel singers who fail sadly in the more exacting demands or the technique of singing of John Sebastian Bach ; while artists for such works as *Messiah*, *Elijah*, and so on, rarely portray that temperament and style which a true presentation of Verdi's great *Requiem* demands. Then, too, a quartet of voices for *Messiah*, or any oratorio, should be of as even quality, quantity, and tone as is possible.

A conductor must have no preference for any one artist or artists, but should always carefully study the demands of the work.

I have noticed during the last few years how dreadfully vibrato is creeping in, and is going to ruin the singing of our choral societies, particularly in the sopranos; even five sopranos with a vibrato in a body of fifty show up, and are most distressing and disturbing to the public in what should be a " still " unison. So please, young conductors, look out for this and nip it in the bud.

In your own studies you will have learned that the breath-taking gaps require time, taken from the last note of the phrase ; and what a help this is to the conductor when he is called upon to become the accompanist on the orchestra ! You will of course place yourself in a position where you are able to *watch the singer's mouth*, and then with that little upward anticipatory stick-gesture you will indicate the necessary breath-gaps, and so prevent your players from rushing onwards and giving no time for that purely human requirement of breathing. I have often noticed how utterly unaware are some conductors of the fact that a singer has to breathe, and, what is worse, the poor singer has either to lag behind the beat or take catchy breaths, which ruin all *quality* of tone and completely upset the vocal line and possibly the phrasing.

Many conductors do not, I fear, realise that it is more difficult to direct perfectly such an aria as Rossini's " Una voce poco fa " than say " The Prize Song " from *Die Meistersinger* ; but you, my conductor with your knowledge of singing, will realise and be able to follow the tempo rubato in which the old Italian arias abound. A conductor should be able to feel instinctively these requests, and direct *with* the singer or instrumentalist ; but alas, it is so often a case of, as I say, the four-square beat which regrettably *defeats any real artist*, or that dreadful catching-up beat which is never with the artist but always trotting up behind.

The art of directing recitative seems to me to be a lost accomplishment, possibly because the day of the great singer has been allowed to lapse since the solo pianist has caught the public's fancy. Recitative, if rendered correctly, is an accomplishment which reveals not only the artist, but dramatic intelligence ; and I regret beyond words the elimination of *true* recitative, not only in the present-day renderings of oratorio, etc., but also in opera. I recently attended a performance of a delightful opera—splendidly produced and dressed, backed by a vivid and accurate translation from the original tongue, which musically was utterly spoiled because all the recitatives were *spoken*, and not sung as written. This is all wrong, and I hope intelligent singers will start afresh and restudy the great singers of opera, via gramophone records, if they are uncertain of this accomplishment. Why on earth some conductors persist in beating out the full bar in strict time in accompanying recitative, I cannot understand. Give freedom to the singer's interpretation and the sense of the story he has to tell, and the artistry of your baton will guide your orchestra ! Learn the words of any aria yourself beforehand ; I can assure you it will be such a help.

Point VIII.—The Conductor must have a good physique, a good temper, and a strong sense of discipline.

In Point VII I lay stress on the value of the study of singing as of supreme help in building up the diaphragm through the act of correct breathing, and on its value to the would-be conductor. I cannot emphasise this point too much. If you can once master the only true method of deep breathing then you will find yourself unflagging and tireless throughout both rehearsals and concert. I believe too that a tight abdominal belt (correctly measured and made) is most helpful in assisting and supporting the upward effort of breath so essential.

A little story attaches to this upward effort of breath. Having heard Jean de Reske sing as a baritone, I was greatly surprised to hear him some years later as the glorious tenor we shall always remember in connection with opera—and what a singer he was ! Well, he had studied carefully the art of breathing and found that by tightening the waist-line below the base of the lungs, he could support that upward pressure of breath on which to sing ; and in this way he gradually pushed his voice up and up until he became the tenor of that supremely effortless style and tone quality which was sheer joy to listen to. If you see photographs of Patti, Melba, Jenny Lind, and such singers, you will note the small waist-line—no low abdominal breathing in these great singers—and you may rest assured that they would not have succumbed to a mere fashion ruling at the time at the expense of their art, but rather that the fashion of those times happened to assist the art of singing. (Always remember that singing is an effort of breath, not of voice !) I am convinced that singers of the present day could add many notes to their compass if they would only adopt the tightened waist, and spend a few months on learning to breathe correctly ; they would lose that shocking wobble and tremolo that seems to attack so many.

This breath control is absolutely essential in the case of the conductor. It supports the continual upward lift of the arms, and you don't get " out of breath," never mind how energetic the call on your powers. The arms appear to be lighter, a fact which you can test for yourself. Clasp your waist-line with both hands from each side, take a deep breath and hold the hands tight, then breathe upward and out very slowly. When you have learned to do this, take in your breath without the hands clasped at waist and raise your arms in a gesture of conducting, and you'll find a support and lightness, quite untiring, as opposed to the flabby outward and downward abdominal breathing.

A sense of discipline is absolutely essential. The conductor's life should be one of self-discipline first and last. It is hopeless to think you can play tricks with your health and keep up to the great strain of a busy conductor's life. All my life I have set myself a rule guided entirely as a means to an end. I have never allowed myself the pleasures of a supper out after a concert, except on very rare occasions, or lunching in party-fashion prior to a concert; never a late night if a rehearsal is booked for the morrow morning, and so on. And as for wine and such good things, these always in strict moderation, and not *at all* during the hours preceding rehearsal or concert. Mark you, I should be the last to advocate a " dry " policy. The good things—good food, good wines, a good cigar—all refresh when taken at the right time. In fact, I can hardly imagine an interpretative musician who does not understand and require the rehabilitation that good food and good wine provide. But watch it, my young friends ; your health comes first, and a conductor's job is an exacting mistress from A to Z. You cannot tackle any job, especially that of directing an orchestra, the morning after the night before. This self-discipline is all important, because you must be on top when facing a body of 90 or 100 players. They may have been out the night before, and may not be feeling musically very fresh or alert ; but the conductor has got to be " the big man," and a look from his eye should inspire and help to give musical feeling even to tired and fatigued players. You must remember ninety odd units go to make " The Orchestra," and every unit is a human being ; each has his, or her, own particular mood and circumstances—home worry, a binge a late bus or train ; a hundred and one elements are brought together to sink their personal identities in " The Orchestra." If the conductor is not on top from the moment he mounts the rostrum, he cannot hope to merge the varied interests into a workable whole ; your rehearsal will prove, if not useless, unenlightened.

The players are quick to note a mood in their director, and quick to respond to *inspiring* requests ; while niggling grumbles and grousings, which are the usual outcome of the undisciplined hours, merely throw the player back into his own particular little bit of worry or " liver."

Self-discipline gives personal confidence, and the courage so requisite if your will and direction are to be superimposed on a body of musicians. A great deal has been said and written about the conductor " ruling his players," but my experience teaches me that a first-rank conductor exercises control by the respect and confidence the orchestra places in him, and far from " ruling," his method is to coax and persuade the answer he wants. You must practice control and avoid personal preferences ; you should be able to insist on a point of discipline without rancour. You may be called upon to settle many questions of orchestral etiquette. You may find yourself obliged to " tick off " a player for inattention : all kinds of tricks happen behind desks, which the conductor is not supposed to see—and if he's wise, he doesn't see— until the particular piece of inattention is leading to a departmental joke at the expense of efficient rehearsal.

I must admit that the general sense of discipline is less evident in 1943 than it was in the days of my Queen's Hall Orchestra, for it is nothing now-a-days for a wind player to miss a cue, because he is reading his daily paper or smoking a cigarette, head well down, hidden as he thinks behind his desk. Of course we shall always have the lazy player, but in the days of the Queen's Hall Orchestra they didn't get the chance, for the manager's (Robert Newman) keen eye was watching from the circle during every rehearsal. He would come down to me and say : " Do you think that second violin at desk 4 is carrying his weight ? " or " Is that new viola player all right ? " So many players are apt to think you don't notice the little antics they get up to, to avoid going all out during a rehearsal. And again, if you are wise, you won't see the violin player who is persistently cleaning his glasses, or admiring the shape and colour of his instrument, or making a study of the latest prices on a race, or the wood-wind player keen on the investments' summary ; until you feel it is time to let him know you have him " taped," and this you do so quietly through pointedly directing at that desk.

Remember that you *must* exercise control, first of all through impeccable musical knowledge and decisive beat, and remember that when verbal direction is necessary, it must be *to the point*. Never irritate your players (especially if you happen to be a young man facing a body of good old seasoned players) by talking ; they hate to be lectured to no purpose, and the " talky " conductor usually presents these old stagers *gratis* with his want of experience, and possibly, of knowledge.

You must never allow elasticity in attending your rehearsals. If a rehearsal is called for 10 a.m., 10 a.m. should see you on the rostrum ready to commence. Never permit a deputy to attend your rehearsal, to be replaced by the regular player at the next rehearsal for the concert, or at the concert should only one rehearsal be called. This is a sore point in orchestras, for although I fought the deputy system in 1904, it still rules today, and I know some of the managements of the orchestras undergo many harassing hours endeavouring to keep their team loyal to the organisation. It is such a pity, for the first essential to a permanent orchestra is permanent personnel. I must say since that break-away in 1904, when

the disputants left me and formed themselves into the London
Symphony Orchestra, I have not suffered from this disastrously
unprincipled habit, thank goodness. It is of course all a
matter of £ s. d., which the following letter from my old
friend John Solomon, the trumpeter, goes to show, which he
wrote on the occasion of my conducting Jubilee in 1938 :—

1st October, 1938.

Dear Sir Henry,

I cannot let this opportunity pass until I have sent
you my sincere congratulations on attaining your
Jubilee. I have seen the *Radio Times* and read the
article you have written. As one of your boys I appreciate all you have done, not only for me but for all our
late players who are gone, in those days when we were
first associated at Q.H. and the splendid times we had
with you. Myself, I have always had the greatest
admiration of you, or for you, and fortunately never
crossed words. I see in the article you mention the
break-away from you 34 years ago. I don't know
whether you have ever had the history of that break.
May I be allowed as a culprit to tell you how deeply
sorry we were for it, but the real truth is that all our
old players built up a connection such as best concerts,
festivals and many other engagements which we had
been forced to accept, not knowing what would happen
for the future, as when you made such a success after
a few years, you might have been snapped up either
abroad or elsewhere, and the Q.H. orchestra would have
been abandoned or smashed up. Consequently we
would have been stranded, both Q.H. and outside
engagements. So we consulted together and the four of
us Founders (Flounders) started to work to form the
L.S.O., Busby being the culprit who made himself

Managing Director. Directly we had your letter of dismissal something had to be done and the upshot were meetings and the L.S.O. was formed. I won't trouble you further as you know the rest. I was very upset at the time leaving you because I was happy in my work and position as Principal with you and have been the same since at the R.A.M. and hope to continue. Now I can only say I am pleased to write and hope again that you may be spared to go on for many years to come with health and vitality that you have shown to all in your career, and those who have come in contact with you.

Believe me to always remain,

Yours sincerely,

(Signed) JOHN SOLOMON,

F.R.A.M., F.T.C.L.

If your rehearsal commences badly, players late or uncomfortably seated (I know nothing that annoys a player more), don't get ruffled ; keep calm and keep cheerful above all. The temper and attitude of the conductor matter so much, for players are quick to " sense " the right mood and will respond or not in even measure. Never be " pally " with your players ; be friendly of course (I like to feel that orchestral musicians are my friends, as I have been, and am, theirs), but once on the rostrum you should be in a position to command the respect which undue " palliness " is apt to diminish. If you are young and have the natural feeling of diffidence coupled with a little wholesome fear, never try to overcome this by currying favour, such as agreeing that because a work is so well known it is not necessary to rehearse it. You will always be up against the problem of the player who requests to be let off early, or from the complete rehearsal ;

but never give way—he is called and paid for that rehearsal, and should be at his post just as you are at yours.

I dislike the term discipline; but because *you* lead a disciplined life, it does not imply a narrow, grudging outlook, and the more you can approach your players in the light of friendliness, interest, and pleasure, then the greater will be their response. This is discipline applied. When rehearsal is about to start, see that all players are at their desks, and see to it, too, that your string players sit well and comfortably with good elbow-room, and never allow players to sit with legs crossed; tone is lost, and it looks untidy as well, and certainly tends to slackness.

Never lose your temper. The day of the prima-donna conductor who breaks his baton and raves at the orchestra is passed. But at times in a busy life you are bound to come up against a difficult patch. I remember once a particularly bad beginning of a rehearsal at Queen's Hall. I simply could not get attention. There had been some " domestic " meeting regarding a purely orchestral disagreement; and after trying calmly and gently I found the meeting virtually in progress among players of the wind department. So, without temper, I merely said : " Well, ladies and gentlemen, you are evidently not here to rehearse this morning, and I am not here to waste my time," and went home to more profitable study.

A point that drives the professional player quite mad is the conductor who is continually stopping " to go back to so-and-so cue " without explaining his reason; they don't mind how many times they are called upon to go back, so long as they are *aware of the reason*. But the conductor who requests them to go back " for my sake, gentlemen," and that kind of thing, is asking for the kind of trouble that only the orchestral player can brew, in the subtle manner that can be *felt* rather than *seen* during a rehearsal—but certainly heard

at the performance. Of this I speak later on in the study of
scores, and the making of your rehearsal lists. Believe me,
an orchestra need not be articulate to show disapproval.
You *see* it, you *sense* it, and you an *feel* it, and when you
find that attitude you may just as well go home. But, my
would-be conductor, you will not be honest to your players,
your public, your management, yourself, and above all
to the composer if you shirk rehearsal of the veriest repertoire
works. Let me tell you this : the orchestral musician
knows whether you avoid rehearsal to curry favour ; while,
on the other hand, if you are young and inexperienced he will
resent your want of discipline, for *he* wants to know what
you are going to do at the performance. The really sincere
orchestral musician is out for the best possible performance
always. So do remember you gain nothing, and tend to
lose both prestige and respect when you endeavour to curry
favour by cutting out rehearsal.

If I had my way I should make it imperative that every
Symphony Concert be given at least nine hours' rehearsal,
as opposed to the three hours for a Promenade Concert.
It is extortionate to extract higher prices for a so-called
symphony concert, if such a concert is given no more rehearsal
than that afforded for a daily Premenade Concert ; and what
is far more to the point an orchestra meeting daily, as they
do during a long Promenade Concert season, eight to ten
weeks on end, attain a proficiency of ensemble not possible
when meeting for one concert here and there under different
conductors. It is time that the public demanded this redress,
and time too that our musicians saw to it that a Symphony
Concert demanded and produced playing equal to the finest
permanent orchestra in America. I should like to institute
one string rehearsal, one wind rehearsal, with one full rehearsal
for every symphony concert. This would assure ensemble
and intonation, and should be quite sufficient for a representa-

tive symphony-concert programme ; but if a new work is
down, then I should like twelve hours' rehearsal, two
departmental and two for full orchestra.   My young-colleague-
to-be, if you see to this in the future, you will be progressing :
don't go back, go on from where I am stepping down ; build
up on what I have built; you can afford to do so, for,
whereas I have had to peg away each year making, teaching,
and educating a public, you now have that public made for
you, and managements can afford to let music go forward,
for we have now beyond question a vast public for serious
music.

This brings to my mind my words on discipline—self-
discipline—which on one occasion in my life I confess to have
ignored.   When Sibelius came to direct on several occasions
during 1921 at Queen's Hall, in the good days when a
Symphony Concert was indeed what it set out to provide—
a programme of music for which adequate rehearsal had been
provided, and a full Symphony Orchestra with adequate
strings (what is one to do with twelve first violins, and so
on ?)—we naturally discussed the works on hand and many
others.   During such chats Sibelius told me he had never
been satisfied with a certain crash chord—it never reached
that deliberation—every player dead on it with all they
have got to give.   Well, I set out to see to it that this must
"come off" whenever I directed this Symphony again.   I did
everything I could to satisfy myself, but only on few occasions
could I feel that I had attained just what my old friend
wanted ; so much depends upon the players—whether they
are fatigued, inattentive, or what you will.

One morning, however, after having listened to a series
of very uninspired concerts (it was 1936, if I remember
rightly), I was fired with redoubled enthusiasm when I
took my stand for rehearsal with the B.B.C. Symphony
Orchestra in preparation for a Symphony Concert (for which

mark, you, twelve hours' rehearsal was properly provided),
and determined to obtain the result Sibelius wanted in the
E flat minor, the Symphony in this programme. Could I?
No! The players were Monday-morning-ish, as only players
can be, and how exasperatingly mulish they *can* be when they
get together in such a mood. Well, I tried and tried but to
no real effective purpose; so left it for another attempt
after the interval. Still I could not get that momentary
lift prior to the chord—no, it wouldn't shape. Again, and
for once in my life I lost my temper, or rather should I say
I allowed my temper to take charge of my gesture, and with
a down beat and all the force of muscle and temper behind it,
still that chord with all the *deliberation* wanted did not come
off: but I tore the ligaments of the upper arm and shoulder.
In much pain I persisted in the schedule of rehearsal, although
I could not lift my upper arm and directed entirely from the
elbow with forearm. The chord did come off at performance;
perhaps sympathy played a part in it, for the orchestra
knew I was suffering. This want of control kept me a
prisoner, with my arm in one of those horrible abduction
splints for many weeks; happily it proved effectual and
the torn muscles healed without complications. This is
demonstration that force, or temper, or both must never
be behind your beat; only the art of using your wrist
action to beat is of any service to you.

I cannot stress too much that care and thought should
be given to the matter of clothing, from both the health
point of view as well as finding it always possible under any
conditions to appear well-groomed and suitably attired.
Some of my colleagues are lucky and don't perspire as I do,
and so their trouble in both instances is greatly lessened.
But if you do or do not perspire, it is essential to good health
that you change all under garments and get a good rub-down
with spirit (I always use good eau-de-cologne), and if

available a cool shower, after rehearsal and concert. I make a point of wearing woollen under-garments always, never mind the temperature, as they absorb moisture and retain warmth, so lessening the chance of chill. My suits for rehearsal are kept entirely for that purpose, and are of pure woollen material, the waistcoat being completely lined back and front (back is most important) with pure woollen lining. Always see that after changing and perhaps packing for home or a journey, this suit is fully aired before wearing it again. When you are not so busy, one suit may perhaps suffice ; but I find at least three rehearsal suits are essential. This is an economy too, for if they are made of the same material repairs are easily effected. I have all garments numbered on each piece, Suit No. 1, No. 2, No. 3, and so on. I have several evening suits built in the same way, and interlined at back with a light woollen material. This again is an economy, and easy for valeting. This may appear to be over-cautious, but I have learnt from the hard school of suffering ; for there was a time when, left much to my own devices to look after myself, I suffered a continual cold and catarrh in the head which at times became so bad that I suffered giddiness when conducting, and this plan has proved its own wisdom. I may add, too, that in keeping a definite wardrobe for your professional work, you are ready at any moment to face your orchestra smartly and properly attired, which in itself gives a personal sense of well-being, as well as offering a compliment to your orchestra in appearing before them in trim, disciplined fashion.

This may all seem beside the point to a young would-be conductor, but I assure you anything you can devise which goes to the equipment of the professional life you hope to achieve, is helpful in creating that atmosphere of detachment and perparedness so essential. Such an attitude is to be commended in any career, but it is much more so, and far more necessary, in that of a professional conductor whose very work is apt to create a Bohemian, happy-go-lucky spirit. So that anything you can do to keep within ordinary bounds a temperament responsive to outside influences is, I assure you, one of the first principles that will hold you in good account with the orchestras you are called upon to direct. Don't mistake me, I would not advocate a prudish, milk-and-water attitude, and my warning is only intended to advise you that the hours you spend before your orchestra are hours which will inevitably seal your future career one way or the other. I know quite well that if you questioned an orchestral player he would say : " Dress ! I don't care what a conductor wears." On the other hand I maintain that we are a people accustomed to a certain manner of dress for certain occasions, and the very fact that we are dressed according to the dictates of the occasion creates a visual impression of being ready for the work on hand with discipline and forethought, and creates also an atmosphere of agreeable settling-down to rehearsal or concert. Studio work is answerable for a great deal of short-comings in this matter, and I deplore so much the growing tendency of players to strip even down to an under-vest when rehearsing, and to remain so before an invited audience during a broadcast concert. Comfort, yes ; but disciplined comfort, and if players have generally agreed that the regulation dress for certain occasions is not comfortable, then new patterns and materials should be devised and agreed upon by their orchestral committees, so that the orchestra presents a workman-like uniform appearance both for rehearsal and performance anywhere.

A further note of warning ; never allow yourself to run the risk of chill by standing about in draughty corridors talking to people after a concert. Change at once and meet your friends afterwards, for a chill the night before might prevent your directing a work the next morning which you have had under rehearsal for six or more hours after weeks of careful study. I speak with authority, for I used to go straight from the platform for a car journey to my home without changing, a matter of time and convenience, which in spite of my care in choice of wardrobe, etc., found me each Promenade Concert season with bronchitis and an everlasting cold and catarrh. Just don't do it, look after your health first.

THE INFINITE VARIETY OF A CONDUCTOR'S DUTIES

The plans referred to appear on end papers to this book.

First and foremost the placing of his orchestra. I print two plans here, by kind permission of Messrs. Boosey and Hawkes, which I provided for their splendid little book *The Orchestra and its Instruments.* I prefer my first and second violins on my left, as from long experience I maintain that by this placing better ensemble is assured, and volume and quality of tone improved with all the S holes facing the auditorium ; the 'cellos and basses on my right, because they too are of a colour, and ensemble is better assured by placing together instruments of the same family.

In arranging the lay-out of the orchestra in a fan-shaped position, the eye of the conductor can take in practically all

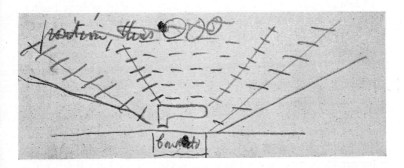

the first and second violins on his left (a very important point to obtain a perfect ensemble) and on looking to the right he can see at a glance all the 'cellos and double basses, and most of the violas. Looking straight in front of his nose, he can take in the full wood-wind players, tympani, etc., with the horns on his left (in this position the bells of the horns are turned towards the public), while the trumpets, trombones, and tuba are on his right.   In placing the wood-wind, draw a straight line from the nose of the conductor to the tympani (drums), and put the first wood-wind players next to the central line right and left, so that you have three each of the woodwind players on either side.

By this arrangement your wood-wind and horns can hear each other and feel in touch with one another, which ensures ensemble and certainly better chordal playing.

Place the harp, or harps, in the centre of the orchestra if possible, just in front of the first flute and first oboe, dividing slightly the violas from the second violins.   In this position they can hear all solos from the wood-wind department and strings.   Placing the harp at the side of the orchestra or behind the 'cellos is a grave error, which I realise cannot always be overcome, as they often have to accompany important solo instruments and from that position hear nothing ; you cannot blame them for poor ensemble if they cannot hear what they are supposed to accompany.

I assure you there is nothing that makes an orchestral player so utterly unmusical as to be seated without sufficient room *all round* him ; there must be no back desk touching his shoulders, no ' cellist's bow touching his partners, no violin bow-arm nudging his partner's elbow, and even the wind departments must have a complete sense of space, if you are to get really good playing.

I have been upset during the past few years by the general tendency to set out our concert orchestra in long lines, on the right and left of the platform.   In Great Britain little or no thought is given to concert-platform arrangements.   The architects never meet and discuss this most important point. In one beautiful new concert hall in the North of England, I measured 72 feet from the last desk of the first violins on the conductor's left, to the first desk of the double basses (old-fashioned placing) on his right. How can your eye, beat, or gesture cater for orchestral musicians thus seated?

While on this topic of construction I do hope that when it comes to equipping the platform of the Proms Jubilee Concert Hall in London, the committee and architect—or whosoever is going to be responsible for the Hall—will get together a number of orchestral players, the "Leader" of *every* department, to decide upon a *standard* chair suitable for his comfort and the instrument he is to play, and a *standard* desk. This is all important.

The conductor's desk too is all important. I have always had my own desk, with a flat top, only just large enough to take an ordinary open score. Those dreadful "writing desks," illuminated if you please, make for an ungainly and unnecessarily wide beat, and the baton is bound to catch the edge sometimes and produce that disconcerting tap, usually at the moment of a sustained pianissimo! Make certain the rostrum is well out; never allow yourself to be in line :—

Violins - - - Rostrum - - - 'Cellos

for this absurd position demands unnecessary movement in bringing in either department, and is showy and fidgety both for the players and audience alike. The rostrum should be dead flat—spirit-level flat in fact; a purely physical precaution, for if the stand slopes even the slightest degree backwards you will find that after a three hours' rehearsal and two hours' concert the back muscles of your legs ache, and this in turn will create hard tightened muscles which bring in train neuritis or arthritis troubles; while if sloping forward, the toes push into the boot most painfully resulting in corns and nail troubles!

Don't be ruled by your orchestral attendant; see to it before the rehearsal starts that he has placed the orchestra to your plan.

Always remember the piano—two or three pianos even—and cater for this emergency in your planning. In accompanying a piano concerto always make sure that you can see the pianist's hands and can catch his eye. It is all very well to be familiar with a certain concerto, but no two artists interpret a work in exactly the same manner (thank goodness !) and if you keep an eye on the hands of the artist you will avoid those unhappy jumpy entrances we hear too often. It is much better to have the artist's cadenza before you during rehearsal and performance, so that you can follow in sympathy with the artist, as the joining-up of the cadenza with the orchestra should be completely dovetailed. If this is left to chance it creates that atmosphere of alert suspense—will it come off ? Actually I should prefer to ask every artist to play through his cadenzas at rehearsal, then the players and conductor have some idea of the length and style, and moment of entry ; but, alas, time is of so much value in a short two-and-three-quarter-hour rehearsal for a concert the same day that this has by custom been dispensed with.

The solo violinist and 'cellist should always be in a position to allow the conductor to keep his eye on fingers and bow ; thus obviously a better ensemble is assured. The same with the singer ; watch the mouth and intake of breath, which will enable you to give that little " breath beat " which is so essential for this purely physical requirement.

The art of orchestral accompaniment does not wholly lie in ensemble, but very largely in the sympathetic under-standing of the instrument or voice, and interpretative sense. Accompaniments to lower voices should always be lighter if possible than for the higher, because the lower octave does not insist over the strings and wind, which in many passages may be playing an octave higher. Piano and violin get through more easily, but the 'cello does not, and I always suggest for 'cello concertos a reduction in the number of players, and even in a large hall desks 5, 4, 3, 2 are more than sufficient; while all else in the orchestra must be kept down. How well members of the Queen's Hall Orchestra will remember Casals, and how he used to hiss if the orchestration was of too much tone and volume to prevent his tone predominating; and dear old Ysaÿe, how he used to exclaim, turning to the players: "Gentlemen, I am but a small violin, not a trombone!"

When directing a piano concerto always have your rostrum high enough to enable your players immediately behind the open piano-lid to see your beat clearly, and insist on a *short* prop stick for the piano-lid support.

It is the conductor's duty—his first and last duty—to see to it that the composer's score is fully carried out. If the composer writes for six horns or even eight, be sure to see to it that you demand them. The same in wind departments; never in these days pander to a management, unmindful of the charge upon you as a serious musician, by boiling down parts or "cutting" in any shape or form. The strings are always too few anyway—even Bach himself made the same complaint in his day—and I wish I could see it made compulsory to have at least 16 first violins in a symphony orchestra, though I could wish it might be 24 at least. It seemed strange to me that, in these days when we have been obliged through circumstances of war, when dear old Queen's Hall fell to enemy action, to give orchestral and symphonic concerts in the Albert Hall—a wonderfully fine hall certainly, but one not acoustically designed for this kind of performance, since string tone and colour are lost in the maze of the echo, which, alas, appears elusive of control— that no one attending that wonderful concert arranged by the *Daily Telegraph* in honour of my birthday appeared to notice the writing on the wall. That concert was an historic musical experience for we had *adequate strings*—the string

departments of the three permanent London orchestras !
Our programme was a short and familiar one which made
adequate rehearsal a simple matter, and both the playing
and the string tone that day made for all real musicians
present an unforgettably beautiful musical experience ; yet
I do not think this was commented upon by the press. Surely
here was a chance to advocate more, and yet more, strings
in the future, for it was substantiated beyond question that
day. Always ask for more and more strings, and in turn it
will be seen it is worth while from both musical and box-
office returns.

Ah, I can hear someone telling you, my young would-be
conductor : " Why, Wood used to boil down his parts to
fit the managements' pockets." Yes, of course I did, but
that was in *the old days long ago when serious music was bound
to be produced at considerable loss,* and I was quite determined
to build up a public by way of the glorious classical repertoire—Beethoven, Brahms, Bach, with Tchaikovsky and
Wagner : that glorious paean of sounds which I hoped to
be able to produce one day, but which I could never have
put into my programmes at that time if I had not made
the score fit my orchestra. Through my pioneer work all
those years past, we are undoubtedly now a nation music-
conscious, and you, my young friend, benefit from my
struggles in dear old never-to-be-forgotten Queen's Hall in
the early days of the now world-famed Promenade Concerts ;
so you have it in your hands now to make of the English
orchestras organisations that are a national asset and second
to none musically.

I cannot speak too feelingly regarding this faith to the
composer. Should you find yourself at any time pledged to
produce a concert that will not cost more than a given figure
for your orchestra, do, please do, compile your programme
within the limits of your orchestra ; for to produce a fine

work without the instruments required simply means you reduce the " sounds " which hold the uninitiated part of an audience, and without which you may possibly turn away from serious music a potential public of some hundreds. Keep your audience always mettled, always wanting more ; and you'll never do it, my friend, with that dry as dust parade of a Tchaikovsky symphony or any other work, in skeleton form. You kill Tchaikovsky, Bax, Bliss, Walton, or what you will, and a potential public in one go—so *never* cut your orchestra.

You must keep an eye on your composer's score too, for I find that *even he* will at times succumb to the enticement of getting a work played by "cutting." I have seen inside a score " this can be performed with so-and-so wood-wind." This is pandering to mean managements, for if a composer truthfully wrote down his vision and thought, how on earth can he expect that work to succeed as it would possibly have done, had he not given permission for such " cutting " merely to get the work performed ? Why did he not write it as he was prepared to *allow* it to be performed ?

Another duty—never make a promise to direct a concert, even though you agree to it, for a charity or from some benevolent intention, unless you keep that promise. You fail in your obligations, first to your personal detriment, and if you are gaining ground, any such lapse may prove your undoing : the public has a habit of remembering. Stick to an engagement, never mind what tempting work may intervene ; and I can speak feelingly on this subject, for I have year after year, in the early days of my Promenade Concerts, refused offers, tempting musically and more so financially, to direct abroad just when I should be here getting ready the programmes and the thousand-and-one details of my Promenade Concerts. To all I have turned a deaf ear in the interests of the work to which I had already pledged my service. I cannot say the result is disappointing—it is thrilling and a life's dedication established. They say a man is as good as his word ; bear this in mind, my would-be conductor, for now, more than ever, you have a music-wise public with whom sincerity counts quite a lot. This reminds me that when still quite a young man, but getting on—my fees having reached the ten-guinea mark—I learned that a certain well-known and well-to-do composer-conductor was directing concerts for a like fee ! " This is not good enough," said my father; " go and see him, and tell him so ! " I did, and I must say he was very charming, for I knew him well. When I reminded him that if *he* directed for ten guineas, how on earth was I ever to ask and reach the twenty-guinea mark, he replied it was a point of view he had not considered, but added : " It shan't happen again, my boy " ; and I am quite sure he stood by this promise.

To the conductor usually falls the choice of programme and artist ; in fact I do not undertake to direct a choral work unless I am satisfied with the singers for a given work.

In directing an oratorio with chorus, orchestra, and solo singers, the conductor must never forget that he is there for the purpose of co-ordination and ensemble, and not to predominate the whole. In preparing any choral performance the conductor should meet his choir months ahead as many times as possible as that his particular reading may be carefully studied and perfected. In every instance the conductor should have piano rehearsals with his solo singers long before the date of performance so that exchange of views in the interpretation may be decided long in advance. A conductor must remember that a singer has made a careful and long study of the part, and that any last-minute change is of very grave consequence to a vocalist. In fact, providing a singer is musically correct, I do not agree with imposing your own personal interpretation any more than you would think of instructing a pianist or solo instrumentalist, and you could do this with conceivably less harm, for once a singer has a work " placed " in his voice, with expression and phrasing, it is positively devastating to endeavour to remould the rendering at a rehearsal on the day of performance, and somewhat of an unwarrantable intrusion of opinion if suggested even weeks before. I have never understood why singers should be treated as a class requiring instruction while solo instrumentalists commit equal variations of style or faults without comment from the conductor ; and yet to unmould a singer's interpretation is far more harmful to that delicate instrument—the human voice.

A conductor should always remember in responding to applause after a choral performance that his solo singers, his choir, and his orchestra share in this tribute, and he should see to it that both chorus and orchestra respond by rising, while solo artists with himself receive the final acknowledgments. In a purely orchestral work, of course, there is not so much need for the more impersonal acknowledgment of applause. A conductor should in fact see to it that by implication or intent he does nothing to intrude himself upon an audience—he is there always for the purpose of co-ordination and ensemble in the reading of a composer's requests; and even though his interpretation excels, he could not have done it without the complete co-operation of his players. The man who " plays to the gallery," or attracts attention by artificial methods, may get away with it once, but I assure you, any method of public performance that savours of showmanship rather than musicianship and sincerity is soon found out and mistrusted. Once a conductor is afflicted with limelight fever, you may rest assured the music suffers, and he does eventually. I have gone to some pains to advise you on this point, my would-be conductor, for I find so many young students of music assume that flashy demonstrations get over the footlights, and that the conductor's position in front of an orchestra is an easy means to that end.   But don't you believe it, for a conductor of any real and lasting worth is a sincere musician whose life is given up to the music with no thought of self in presenting it.

A dozen other factors attack the solo artist, instrumental or vocal, at the moment of interpreting a solo or concerto. We never know what worries they may have gone through at home or business, or how ill they may feel at the moment ; but it must not show in their work, and this calls for courage and is a great nerve strain.   All the greatest artists in the world give bad performances at various times, some go " right off " for a year or two, some never recover.   I can recall bad periods in the lives of many of our great public artists.   I am always a little envious of the literary man, the painter, and even the composer, because a painter, for instance, if he does not feel " painterish " today, tomorrow, or this week, simply does not paint; but a solo artist has to be ready with a work one particular afternoon or evening. Do remember this, my young would-be conductor, when you have attained your goal and are called upon to accompany solo artists.

In preparation for a choral concert a conductor must see to it that all his orchestral parts agree in bowing and marking with his directions to the chorus, so that when all three elements meet on the day of performance, no time is wasted in adjusting such details.   Nothing is so tiring to both singers and orchestra as this continual stopping, which must be avoided at all costs.   Of course it is so much to be wished that every choral performance could be approached with a full rehearsal for chorus and orchestra the day before the concert, and with the solo singers the day of the concert. All these choral societies are composed of amateur singers unaccustomed to the confusing sounds of the orchestra, and some of your singers have to be placed near to instruments that are anything but helpful to them—the percussion and drums for example. This preliminary rehearsal gives them confidence to sing on the morrow with more freedom and conviction. Our great music Festivals instanced this, for rehearsal formed the larger part of the proceedings always, and that is why they were worthy of the title of *Festival*.

The conductor must know by heart the words of the work sung, otherwise he cannot cut off his chords with the final consonants; and, most important of all, the anticipatory breath-taking beat must be very clean. Further he must get *smiling, happy colour out of his choristers* : this is essential. Think of the gloomy, dull, breathy quality you incessantly hear from our choral societies ; never once a smiling, bright, living tone ; anxiety and gloom seem to prevail, especially when they don't know their work very well and do not look the public in the face. It is shocking to watch the down-cast eyes of most choristers. Roy Henderson is right when he insists on his choir singing without music. Vocal colour is otherwise never attended to, and joy, pleasure, interest, and real drama rarely portrayed, and certainly never reflected in the expression of their faces : love, death, sorrow, and "please-pass-the-mustard" all sung in the same colour and with the same facial expression because they do not memorize their work. Never save yourself on choral rehearsals ; take as many as they will give you and more if possible. Make your singers acquainted with the story they have to unfold, read the text to them with correct inflexion and sense of words : paint the picture in fact before you endeavour to set it on the voice. Endeavour to get your singers to sing from memory and so keep their heads out of the vocal score. Just watch a choir and you will possibly find that you rarely see their faces above the backs of the scores ; then how can sound—volume and quality—get through at all ! I always rehearsed Beethoven's 9th Symphony in flats until the last two festival rehearsals. Of course I could write a book on choral conducting, but as this little volume is merely one of advice in setting out on a career of conducting, I can only touch the fringe—not even that far to be of great assistance.

TRANSLATIONS

You will be called upon to direct arias and choral works sung in English, translated from the German, French, Italian, and so on, and will suffer as I have done from wonderfully poetical and cultured translations, where knowledge of music and the human voice is nil, or very elementary. The phrasing is altered, the vocal line lost, and many words placed on a high note impossible to articulate in that position. I could wish that every one about to translate for the singing voice would first of all go through the work with a master of the art of singing ; it may curb your poetical outpouring for a bit, but when you do put your pen to paper after consultation and guidance from this expert in the art of singing, you will find you have happily placed your words on the voice in a way that is capable of telling the public what you are talking about, as well as retaining the composer's vocal line.

My dear young conductor, I cannot too strongly advise you to carefully " revise " any such translation you find your singers are unable to articulate. Don't be afraid to meddle with such translations ; your singers have to enunciate clearly first ! If people who set about making translations from the original tongue in which the work is written would either make themselves proficient in the art of singing first, or seek expert advice, we should avoid some of these horrible contortions utterly impossible for a singer ; they should always remember that when words are set in the original tongue on a certain note, especially if it be in the higher register of any voice, their translation should make every endeavour to retain the vowel or other sound. *Glad* for the German *bahn* is fairly reasonable ; but even so, just sing it for yourself and see how easy it is to sing *b-ahn* on a top note by just closing the lips and opening wide—almost one movement, whereas *glad* on that same top note will certainly become *glard*, a distortion almost impossible to avoid, and if you do avoid it you will get that pinched tone and quality that makes a flat ugly sound, *gled*.

BATON AND BEAT

The mere act of beating time, as I have said before, is comparatively simple, and can be readily assimilated providing you go to some one who can teach you, first, *to hold your baton correctly*, and secondly, is able to instruct you in the *professional* manner to beat time *clearly, very clearly*. My father knew Schulz-Curtius very well ; he ran all the great German orchestras, and it was through him that I got to know Levi, Mottl, and Richter. No one ever directed the *Parsifal* Prelude as well as Levi ; never shall I forget his direction at Queen's Hall at a Schulz-Curtius " Wagner " Concert— it was simply superb. Of course Mottl was just as great in certain works : who will ever direct the Trauer-March from *Götterdämmerung* like Mottl?—the grip, grandeur, weight, and dignity were simply overpowering ! I had the inestimable advantage of discovering with these three conductors so many points in the great symphonic masterpieces. I shall never forget Hans Richter calling at my parents' home one day, at 185, Oxford Street, and talking about Brahms's First Symphony. He borrowed one of my batons, and sitting on our sofa told me how firm his 6-8 two beats in a bar were in the first Allegro ; he never allowed the strings to slip their dotted crotchets, and his up-beat was as firm, clear, and distinct as his down beat. It was from him that I learnt to give a distinct wrist-pulse to my up-beat, in real big heavy stuff. Of course Nikisch had the greatest talent of all the conductors of this period, but it was always Nikisch, and he used his baton more emotionally than anybody else, and of course his tempo rubato was terrific at times. But whatever he directed, he *made it sound so musical, so fascinating* : he certainly did not let the music " speak for itself."

The first fundamental principle to be completely mastered is the method of holding the stick in such fashion as a bow is held, lightly between thumb and first finger. Easy you think ! Try it, and learn to pick up your baton naturally.

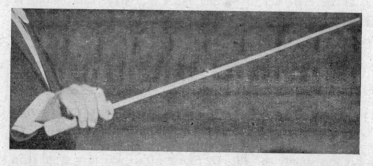

To learn to beat time is a matter of continued practice ; but I cannot say too definitely that you will never carry an orchestra with you unless your beat is decisive and utterly clear. A professional orchestra may get on with an indecisive beat, but you try it on an amateur body of musicians and you'll know where you are at once. I have watched a conductor beating the simple two-in-a-bar measure merely by pointing his baton twice in a left-hand direction across his chest with a round upward swing, denoting a half circle, and being quite surprised that the professional musicians under his direction failed in some chordal passages ! I won't say that a professional orchestra will not manage under any old kind of beat—in time; but if you watch this kind of performance you will note that the leader, if he knows his job as most of them do, will *literally lead* the orchestra.

But you, my young would-be conductor, have to begin at the beginning, and I assure you that if you are determined to apply all the musical knowledge I have indicated, and on it are determined to build your career, your *beat* matters perhaps more than anything. When you go before your orchestra with your carefully studied score and parts, *marked by yourself* according to your interpretation, and can direct with a clear unmistakable *beat*, you have the ear of your orchestra; but once a professional orchestra meets a youngster whose beat mystifies them, they'll let him know it in no uncertain manner, and his first essay is perhaps his last.

I use a particular baton devised to meet what I deem essentials. I began when very young (as most people do) by using a short white stick without a handle, and should in all probability have gone on using the same pattern had I not found that my hand and fingers suffered from cramp when directing an opera every night—a kind of writer's cramp which bothered me for some years. It was Hans Richter who one day, in talking with me and my father in my home at 1, Langham Place (having come from Manchester to ask me to take on the direction of the Manchester Gentlemen's Concerts, from which he was about to resign), advised me to discard this stick for one with a good-sized handle; because, he said, you will find that the continued strain imposed upon the muscles of your hand and wrist by the daily close grip of the finger and thumb will create a kind of neuritis. "I had it," he said, "and found that the solution was a fairly large handle." I was always on the alert for information, and as this came from a man of wide experience and of an age of the giants in music, of which Richter was almost the last of a tradition in conductors, I lost no time in applying his advice. I found a handle on a very short stick unwieldy and ugly, and caused a want of flexibility which was not in keeping with my manner of use of the stick from the first; so to my handle I lengthened

the stick, until I have now still in use the pattern I devised forty years ago.

I may say I have never since suffered aches or pains in arms or shoulders from the effort of conducting, and I shall always thank Richter for his suggestion. I find the long stick remarkably efficient in saving of arm movement, and in handling a large choir and orchestra; it is visible in a wide beat with considerably less effort than with a short stick. I paint my batons a dull-finish white—white because against the regulation black coat it is prominent to every member of the orchestra, and I avoid a bright finish paint as this catches the light in movement and is disconcerting to the players, although of course enamel finish wears better and keeps clean. A 6d. pot of Chinese white, with a good small paint-brush always handy, is a good wrinkle. Your baton must be visible not only to your orchestra, but to the public, who are now so orchestrally-minded, I am thankful to say, and who are quite wise to the art of gesture and so intelligent critics of results attained. By this do not for a moment confuse legitimate gesture and stick movement as being anything in thought or design but the mere directions to the orchestra; for as I have said so often, the flashy conductor who "conducts" for the gallery is soon discovered and known for what he is worth! But now that we have such an understanding and critical public, it is helpful to them, and to musicians, in increasing this enthusiasm, to allow them into our secrets of gesture and direction—and they'll soon see whether the conductor gets what he requests!

I use a cork-handled baton, for the stick must be very lightly held between the thumb and first finger—so lightly poised (I cannot call it held) that any very smooth surface would not provide the delightfully safe contact of cork; moreover, even with my cork handle I have sometimes sent my baton literally into the orchestra, so what fun I might have provided had I used a polished handle I tremble to think, for there can be no gathering of human elements more ready for a joke at the inappropriate time than our dear musicians when banded together as an orchestra! I always keep two batons on my desk for such an emergency, or in

case of one breaking. Mine rarely break in the air; sometimes of course a flaw not apparent is already in the wood
and it will snap with the upward lift even, but more often
such mishaps occur when the piano lid is raised and placed
so near the rostrum that the tip of the baton just snicks it,
and off goes the stick.

I have had my batons made for many years by a firm in
Great Yarmouth, Palmer's. It came about that one of those
interested in that firm, a diligent follower of all the fine
Norwich Festivals of those days, asked permission to make
them for me, and so they have ever since. Here is the
specification of my batons as expressed in a letter from
Messrs. Palmer, Ltd. :—

"WEIGHT : Slightly under 1 ounce

LENGTH of exposed Shaft	19 inches
of Handle	5 ,,
TOTAL LENGTH	24 ,,

SHAFT made of seasoned straight-grain poplar wood,
carefully rived by hand to ensure that the grain
runs straight. Painted white with two coats of
water paint. The shaft runs right through the
handle.

HANDLE of cork 5 inches long, diameter at base
$1\frac{1}{4}$ inches, diameter at shaft end $1\frac{1}{8}$ inch.

"The first one was made in 1921 or 1922 in lancewood.
Sir Henry asked us to make some for him. After a
time he enquired whether we could make them lighter.
We experimented with both willow and poplar, and
finally selected the latter, of which the batons have
been made ever since.

"The batons are not quite so light and pliable as
formerly as Sir Henry wished the size of the handles
increased, and the diameter of the shafts had to be made

slightly larger also to correspond. This increased the weight from just over half-an-ounce to just under an ounce.

"The batons are all made to balance exactly at the shaft end of the handle."

How I wish I could take in hand every young conductor to instruct him in baton technique, and above all the correct way in which to hold the baton! It should be handled as a feather, and my method between the first finger and the thumb excludes the necessity of any obvious movement when a more emphatic beat is required. With the baton poised as I use it, it is a flexible, not a flabby instrument of direction, and that is all important to your musicians. You can do as much with the point of your baton, once you have learnt to wield it, as any great painter can do with his brush; but alas, your mastery and artistry are fleeting and momentary—they may live in the memory only whereas a painter's inspiration lives for all time. I always say I paint the picture with the point of my baton, and I am sure any orchestral player will tell you that I have never left him in any doubt as to my direction—even though I had not a left hand. This again cannot be taught, and I hardly think is quite simple of assimilation, for it is the natural expression of emotion through the act of gesture, derived from the natural outcome of the picture the music conjures in your mind.

To beat time is a comparatively simple thing, and about the only part of conducting which can be taught by individual or class instruction. But I do beg of you, don't go to a man for instruction just because he has a " name," for there are, I am sure, many conductors up and down the country who have no such recognised " name," but who could give instruction and guidance of the greatest value to a young student, and who possess a good stance, a flexible and distinctive beat, and withal a warm enthusiastic musicality. Contact with one of these would be truly helpful.

In this flexible poise of your baton lies ninety-nine per cent. of your ability to direct your orchestra. The secret of this flexibility is that you can with the most simple movement direct the point of the stick to a player whose entry it is; and what a comfort this is to your players who have to sit through long sections of silent bars, and a distinct comfort, too, to make this a rule, for then you run no risk of losing a " lead." But even with all my care in bringing in my players, I have often been obliged to sing a flute or oboe part at the top of my voice lest the clarinet or bassoon, as the case may be, would also go astray without the " cue voice " beside them !

PREPARATION AND STUDY OF ORCHESTRAL SCORES

This is somewhat a difficult matter to write about in definite terms of advice, for every one has some particular preference regarding time and method, but nevertheless a certain amount of routine and discipline is much to be desired. I have always digested a new score from careful reading as a first go-off. I then ask the composer to see me, and go through his work on the piano, carefully noting everything he wishes and where, although marked, it is difficult to convey just that finesse which no musical character can indicate—a *subtle* tempo rubato, a hundred-and-one little points all noted from your quiet study. Absolute quiet and repose are essential to good thinking, therefore your study should be shut away from noise as far as is practically possible. The next thing to do is to " time " the work.

I then conduct through the movement, or work, with my stop-watch. Having decided *your* time for each movement, overture, or short work, put it carefully down for future reference. Having absorbed the work in this way, "listen" to the scoring, detect a weak spot where a wood-wind line will be lost if the other instruments are too strong, and so on ; watch for that theme, that vocal line, try to visualise from eye to ear the picture your composer depicts. Mark your score carefully, and then see to it that the parts agree. I rarely use the piano for such study, and I am sure the eye-to-ear picture is the safe and sure method of capturing and retaining the composer's intentions.

This timing business is to-day a very real necessity now that broadcasting demands there be no silence from 7 a.m. to 11 p.m. or some such time ; it is not an ideal musical alliance, but a very real necessity if you are to get through your rehearsals and concerts before the microphone. One of the most distressing happenings is to be cut off the air at the last few bars of a symphony or other work—anything in fact ; and here is a word of warning. Keep up your sleeve a couple of minutes to spare on a work—even more, on a longish work ; you can always take up the time between movements, but you can't get any tacked on, should the announcer be a little more descriptive than you had anticipated, and you are asked to "hurry up the last move- ment " in consequence. I often wonder whether some of the brightening-up I hear over the air under the direction of men who can be trusted to know the more or less traditional tempi of certain repertoire works, owes the speed to such last- minute requests ! On the other hand I recently listened to a broadcast of Tchaikovsky's Fourth Symphony, and a few days later the Fifth, and I fear I was left in no doubt that neither conductor knew anything of the Russian *mood* or else that they had determined to Americanise it, for the tempi had no relation to Tchaivovsky's requests, much less to the tradition of the Russian race. They are a slow dignified deliberate people, courteous and of much culture, and Tchaikovsky depicted this in all he wrote. Why! I have heard that delightful waltz movement taken at such a speed that you failed to hear any orchestration (and what orches- tration that is !), much less could the wood-wind articulate it—just a blur and so vulgar. Mind you, I say again this business needs your careful study, unless you are to become a Robot—and any metronome could do it better. Give yourself time in hand, always remembering that however familiar you may be with the work on hand " every perfor- mance should be grand improvisation," and if you are a cultured and serious musician, you will of course have analysed Arthur Nikisch's expansive and expressive way of uttering a warning, and realised that " improvisation " as he meant the word was sound advice to approach every work you are about to direct, never mind how familiar, with clear, fresh, and thoughtful preparation ; not for a moment must his meaning be confused with a literal interpretation of the word ! Some of these excesses in tempi, not only in Tchaikovsky's works, but in many of the classics, are indeed horrible improvisations in a very literal sense.

I have found my piano rehearsal with composers of most illuminating character study. One of the most painstaking is Bax, and so was dear Rachmaninoff. I remember when I wanted to give an authentic performance of Rachmaninoff's Third Symphony in 1938, he came to my home and gave me two hours going through the work on the piano ; two hours chock full of interesting and intensive study, marking my score with a precision I could not better, which remains for all time, again proving that genius is the art of taking pains. Bax is wonderfully thorough and *knows* just what he wants— unlike many composers. I have very vivid recollections of a certain composer who bothered me to death prior to the production of a new work of his. He came to the preliminary rehearsal, took his score away, and made certain alterations. The next rehearsal he determined he did not like it, and returned to the original score ; in this he wanted a *subito-piano* before a tremendous crash chord—almost such a chord as I wanted in Sibelius No. 1. I worked at this (in the days of the Queen's Hall Orchestra) until it was perfect, and then, believe me, at the final rehearsal he decided he *didn't* want the *subito-piano* approach ! Well, Bax is not one of these composers, thank goodness. His score is always logical though extremely intricate, but he never misses a point. Of course Bax never directs a work himself, and I think many a composer would be better advised to leave his work in the hands of a conductor he can trust, for obviously his rare journeyings into the directing of an orchestra leave much to be desired, and therefore give a less professional approach, and often an incomplete answer to his work.

The study of the classics can be achieved in many ways, and in these days far more easily than in my young days, when the only means was hearing the actual orchestra during a given performance ; hence my globe-trotting in furtherance of my education. To-day, my young would-be conductor, you have the daily method open to you of " listening " to the orchestras over the air, the much perfected gramophone records, the facilities of travel whereby foreign orchestras are available which you can visit during your vacation, and the number of really first-class orchestras permanently in England. I must stress, however, that there are no two ways about it, and that the actual orchestra, either in rehearsal or in concert performance, is the only perfect method of gaining an introduction to the orchestral repertoire. Always take your score with you, and make it part of your training to go anywhere and everywhere to hear the different readings of a given work under various conductors. Keep notes of all, and as time goes on and your own sense of interpretation grows, you will know just what you want to say—just the tempi you consider right and, in fact, the tone and quality of certain passages on certain instruments.

In getting familiar with the classics via the microphone you must always remember that there is an element of distortion which as yet cannot be eliminated. In fact if you listen carefully, as I so frequently do, you will miss much of the inner harmonies, and especially the bass, over the air. One cannot always blame the conductor, for we have to remember that many and various factors have to be taken into consideration which account for mutilated reception—your receiving set and the building in which it is housed, your personal ability to tune in correctly, the building from whence the music is put over, adjustment of microphones and the human element in the controls' room, and the fact that the man at the controls can raise or lower the volume of sound so often explains the lack of variety and expression which surprises us, when we know who is on the rostrum. Then again, tempi may or may not be quite correct over the air, expecially when a conductor is told just before a performance that his reading of a given work has taken a minute or so more than so and so, when it was last timed, and so he must ", hurry it up " or be faded out. This does not so often happen as to matter to an experienced listener, but my young would-be conductor-listener should always remember this possible contingency, and make it his duty to study this work again in a concert hall.

Regarding gramophone records as an aid to study of the repertoire, I consider this perhaps the most helpful of all, because you can return to them at will, and remember there rarely is a recording put on the market unless made by a fine established orchestra directed by the recognised conductors of the world. If you purchase a given work directed by every conductor available, you can study tempi, tone colour, even harmony and interpretation quietly and carefully until you have formed your own conclusions and decided upon your personal interpretation. The same applies to recorded music as to broadcast, that at times inner harmony and bass are weak, and of course nearly all recordings of orchestral works are apt to be a shade faster than the conductor's tempi would have been in the freedom of a public performance, for he has possibly had to speed up some sections to get a certain part on to a record. Even ten or twenty seconds' speeding up means loss of a certain amount of truth. As an aid to memory the gramophone record is of inestimable value to the young man approaching this career. Don't mistake me, both the wireless and the gramóphone are in their various ways a splendid means of education to the more advanced student. I find gramophone records extremely helpful in checking points I may have criticized from the nearness of the rostrum, if I have been unable to hear a work from the auditorium.

If you are not very proficient, I would suggest that in approaching a new score, you first read through your strings, then your wood-wind, and finally your brass and percussion ; by this means you get a grip of the lay-out of the orchestration, and the general form and feeling of the work. Next study the full score, placed at a perspective whereby you can read at once every stave before you, always remembering that it is essential to learn to place your full score at such a distance to suit your sight so that every line is visible at the same time : no dodging of your head up and down in reading. The next stage is being sure of the tempi set ; conduct through the work, mastering any change of time in the given tempi, and so on, until you are familiar with it and the sound it will produce when you come to face your orchestra.

In going through your score in this way you will have discovered any error, doubtful harmony, a slip or badly written note, and will have corrected it (not altered it, mind you) in the score. You must then look through a set of parts and correct them from the score, when you will be prepared to put the work into rehearsal (I hope with the composer present).

Never mind by what means you decide to make yourself completely familiar with a new score, so long as you have fitted yourself by diligent study to undertake the presentation of a new work sincerely, remembering you may be presenting a work on which the composer's past reputation can be frittered away, just as it may be a first or early work on which his future depends. If you prefer your metronome to tick away during your home studies, then let it tick away

(I personally do not agree with this method), providing you don't allow yourself to become a mere Robot; and if you like to learn the work by playing it over on your piano, all well and good, so long as the result produces a musicianly reading and thoughtful presentation.

PREPARATION FOR REHEARSALS

Once a programme is placed in your hands, the first thing to decide is the orchestra you require, and this is determined by the number of wind, brass, and percussion required, as strings remain fairly static (and always too few). You must early advise your management of the exact players required for the programme chosen; as of long experience you will find that committees will make out a programme and hold their pockets in horror when you remind them that you require, for instance, a contrabassoon, or two harps instead of one, or a bass clarinet and four percussion players, let alone Strauss works often requiring eight horns, five trumpets, treble wood-wind and so on, or Shostakovitch requiring a double brass band! There can be nothing so exasperating both for management and conductor if the latter has overlooked this purely routine duty; on the morning of the concert he meets an orchestra incomplete for the programme on hand; and nothing is so much to be deplored as " doing without " certain instruments for which the composer has written, which this last minute survey may demand, as extra wind players do not abound—especially should your concert be in the provinces.

Another point on going over a suggested programme—you must always bear in mind key-relationship, colour, and form, of which key-relationship is the most vulnerable point; for form these days is of less importance than some years past, and it is not uncommon to find two symphonies 'n one programme nowadays. I have known a programme sent from a provincial committee for my approval entirely in the key of E flat. You should always avoid even two items in succession in the same key as it tends to produce monotony, which is difficult to define but which is felt throughout a house full of an otherwise enthusiastic musical public. As I have said, form is a matter of less cut-and-dried custom now, but from my point of view I should always prefer to see a programme compiled thus :—

> Overture
> Symphony
> Concerto or Arias
> Symphonic Poem or Suite

according to length of time agreed for the concert, and no concert nowadays should exceed two hours including the usual interval

Having definitely decided the programme, make out the order in which you intend to rehearse the items. I make a point of taking first the work requiring the largest number of players, so that those not required for future items can be released, leaving a string piece for instance to the last. Do not however regard this thought for wind and extras as anything but a custom, and in no way a fixture, for every player making up the orchestra is there for the duration of your rehearsal if you so require him. In fact you may some-times find it necessary to run through a major work first with every player present, then, if it does not meet your satisfaction, you may decide to go through it again when the full programme has been rehearsed. I adopt this method especially if this first item is a work with which the orchestra is unfamiliar, because I want as much time as I can scrape together, and by getting rid of other items I know then that the rest of the time is free for this desired rehearsal. Not only this, but artists, perhaps singers or pianists, or both, have been called at a certain hour ; and there is nothing so devastating for an artist as to be kept hanging about for perhaps an eight minute aria, while the orchestra is going through what is an acknowledged repertoire work, but which through infrequent performance is unfamiliar to the players. Always be sure to advise such players that you intend going through this work again at the end of the programme, otherwise you will find they are missing when you will perhaps have a good half-hour to spare for the so much required rehearsal.

Then " call " your artist or artists according to the orchestra required for their work ; although in the case of singers avoid as far as possible calling them too early on a winter's morning, as their journey to the hall is not conducive to comfortable singing.

You will always have to be on your guard in the timing of rehearsals. Very often the shortest piece requires the greatest time to rehearse, so that you must learn to give and take by running through familiar items and make time for the more pressing need of the unfamiliar. Here again your complete musical education will prevent catastrophe and muddle at the last minute.

The customary rehearsal is scheduled for three hours, including the right of a quarter-of-an-hour interval. Remember that it is a quarter-of-an-hour, for even though you inadvertently allow it to creep into twenty minutes, your players as a general rule will be reminding you by a display of time-pieces that at 1 o'clock the three hours is up, and those five minutes you gave them at the interval and had counted on catching up, are quite useless in the general inattention and rush to be away. Always remind your players before leaving the platform at rehearsal of the time the concert commences. Always insist that the order in which the items are to be played at the concert be placed on each stand. Of course you will insist upon tuning prior to the opening item, and never proceed to a concerto without tuning to piano or solo instrument.

Always make a point of having a piano rehearsal with an artist *before* the date of the orchestral rehearsal, as by this means you go before your orchestra knowing exactly what to do and so avoid waste of time. I cannot stress too strongly the desirability of making sure of every debatable point before rehearsal. Know just how you intend to direct a work, especially if it is a choral work, or one with many solo passages.

Remember that you cannot direct the " melos " in more than two important parts at one time, but be quite sure in your studies that mentally you know exactly what you are going to direct ; don't leave it to the band rehearsal to find this out. When directing choral works, most of your attention must be given to the choir because they are amateurs and require constant watching and direction if they are to give of their best, whereas the orchestra can generally be trusted to play the accompaniments to choral stuff fairly well, without much attention except of course for ordinary direction of leads, etc., having had a preliminary orchestral rehearsal (I hope !).

By plotting your rehearsal list in advance you avoid wasting the time of your players and get a better result. I suppose the days will never come again as when Robert Newman allotted me separate string rehearsals and separate wind rehearsals. What a splendid idea ! I shall always remember when I produced *Don Quixote* and *Heldenleben* with the Queen's Hall Orchestra at dear old Queen's Hall. I had four rehearsals for strings only (12 hours), and two wood-wind, brass, and percussion rehearsals (6 hours), followed by two full rehearsals, which were a sheer joy to direct because all the parts were technically perfect.

Going back to a rehearsal list* and the order of pieces, I do impress it upon you that although I have always endeavoured to get rid of pieces requiring the larger number of players this is by no means a necessity, but because it has become a privileged custom it appears to some orchestral musicians to be regarded as an essential factor. Well, as you know those players are usually brass, percussion, and harp—and are in consequence highly lucky—since every string player and, except for a purely string piece, wood-wind too are obliged to remain throughout the rehearsal. So never feel bound by custom if you find that the major piece in your programme requires further rehearsal and are uncertain as to how soon you can get through the remaining works on hand to enable you to go through as far as possible that major work again; but be sure when dismissing them from the platform, you remind them of this intention, or you will not find them in the hall.

Plan your big works employing the full orchestra to start your rehearsal; then after the interval your concerto, and lastly your vocal item and string piece. By planning thus many members of the orchestra could be released after the interval, and only players required for your Beethoven scena and Mozart concerto will be required; and by making your last item the string piece the whole of your wood-wind players can be released. I have found this a very workable scheme. Of course the strings have to remain during the whole of the rehearsal, except upon very rare occasions when you have to rehearse Beethoven's Rondino or a Mozart Serenade for Wind Instruments, when you should put this down last on your list and then you can dismiss your strings

---

* Elsewhere Sir Henry Wood made a fuller exposition of this same point, which was ever in his mind. The two versions of his thoughts, which agree in principle but differ in development, are printed here as showing the importance he attached to the proper planning of rehearsals.

before you tackle your wind piece. I have often, when the programme embraced a short wind piece and a short string piece, given two intervals, one to wind players and one to string players, not leaving the rostrum myself from 10 a.m. to 1 p.m., but using these intervals personally for the preparation of the short works. This is a tip worth mentioning, though of rare occurrence.

If your vocalist is singing a big Wagnerian scena, then such an item must go down early (not too early, remember) in the rehearsal list when the full orchestra is there. I always make a point of going through such an aria with the orchestra alone, having in mind of course my previous piano rehearsal with the solo artist, and so knowing exactly how the artist wished to take the tempi, the accents, rubatos, and inflection. In this way I am able to direct without waste of time, and what is more, without undue strain upon the voice. There is nothing more trying for a singer than continual stopping and repetition merely for the sake of the orchestral accompaniment.

During a Promenade Concert season, when I have often done as many as thirty new works and a vast number of unfamiliar works, the preparation is one which requires a consummate knowledge—hence the years of education I advise. You must first of all know your score—know the spots which *technically* will require more attention, and be prepared with a list in front of you of letters and numbers, with pre-bars already marked and counted, for immediate direction to your players.

You will soon acquire the eye-to-mind reading of your score, and be able to decide how long you will have to give to a piece. For instance a work of such intricate writing as Bantock's *Pierrot of the Minute*—although only playing eleven minutes—requires at least a preliminary rehearsal of sixty minutes, and that is not sufficient. While such a work as *Leonora* No. 1, of Beethoven, playing ten minutes, as a *new* work would nowadays require very much less preparation. Of course no difficulty should arise in presenting a new work if it is down for a separate concert—a symphony concert performance or a festival of music—as adequate rehearsal must be given and *can* be given; but during a Promenade Concert Season you have to slip in such odd hours as will be required and can be stolen from purely repertoire works. Even in these days I should wish for three full hours' preliminary rehearsal to be given for such a work as Richard Strauss's *Don Quixote*, with a preliminary piano run-through with the solo 'cellist. And yet of course this wonderfully intricate work figures in the Promenade programmes every season, and is given only at the expense of other works.

This again bids me remind you that you should have a complete acquaintance with the orchestral repertoire. Only with such knowledge can you compile a programme which can be rehearsed for such concerts as the Promenade and other concerts which provide the only rehearsal on the day of the concert, and one that can be *adequately* rehearsed with the more leisurely preparation I hope to see provided for all symphony concerts.

I could write a complete book on the art of rehearsing and rehearsal discipline, but this little talk is more in the nature of a reminder that to become a conductor of sorts you require an all-round sound musical education; but to be the conductor of such an institution as the Promenade Concerts you must be the complete musician, gifted with tact and sense of discipline, with a flair for keeping your finger on the pulse of the public, and with a determination to train your public in the way you want them to go. Unhappily I find a growing tendency these days to dispense with rehearsal—possibly through exigencies of war-time travel conditions, or inexperienced conductors who endeavour to curry favour with the orchestra by " letting them off " ; but whatever the reason this attitude will bring disaster in its train. I have suffered from results of this attitude, and found that when I required adequate rehearsal of a Bach programme, I could feel the atmosphere : ". What ! we rehearse these simple works ! " I could hear them say or rather look to each other. Well, I did rehearse and was obliged to go through a certain movement twice owing to their utter inattention. This created active disapproval which it did not require my experience to note—one lady put her violin down on her lap and held a running conversation with a gentleman-player near-by. That is not all, but quite sufficient to give you a little timely advice. Never " see " such insubordination, but mark it well and remember. In all my long experience I have never met such a situation, and I trust I never shall again. I don't think I will in fact, because there is no doubt the circumstances of war conditions have given places in the orchestras to many quite unworthy of such positions.

ABOUT A MUSIC LIBRARY AND A
LIBRARIAN'S DUTIES

I have already spoken of preparation of your orchestral material after your own careful study of the score, but another duty is this—and I speak feelingly. If you have not your own orchestral material, your instructions during rehearsal will possibly be *overmarked* on hired or borrowed material by your players, obliterating other markings. Always ask the librarian to see to it that all parts are cleared of such markings before returning them to the library shelves. I have suffered agonies of late years since I gave my library to the Royal Academy of Music on condition that it *should* be available for hire (the proceeds going to a fund I instituted for the benefit of necessitous students), and have wasted many valuable moments, in precious rehearsal time, rubbing out over-markings in my own parts, which of course had been carefully marked with all the care I always put into such preparation. You should ask your players to remember your requests as far as possible; if not the orchestral librarian must come to the rescue as I have indicated.

I wonder by the way how many musicians really know what constitutes a music librarian, and what is more, how many realise the value of that folder of music which he finds on his desk in preparation for a concert? I wish all our colleges of music would include a course in music librarianship in their curriculum and make it a condition that every student attends lectures at least once a month on the care and preparation of such material. How often has it been my experience to start rehearsal on a work to find on request for an entrance omitted—say the piccolo, or second flute, or what you will—that that part is missing ; and on enquiry, when I have returned the material to the library, have been told : "Oh, you required only seven desks, first violin, and on going through the parts we have found the missing piccolo (or some such part) inside the eighth-desk violin"! What did I do on such occasions ? Write out the missing part of course, but what a waste of valuable rehearsal time !

Then again a music librarian should be able to make clean and legible repairs, bind and repair backs of volumes. You have no idea how urgent this branch of music is, and what a help and comfort it is to know of a really good working librarian. A word of advice will not be amiss here on this subject, especially now that the permanent orchestras are gradually building up their own music libraries. If you want badly to take up a career in music and find yourself a ready study, but do not see much evidence of that accomplishment which will make you a fine singer, pianist, or instrumentalist, take up the serious study of "librarianship," and possibly learn to use all the percussion instruments, and then you will, I have no doubt, find a ready outlet for your musical ambitions, and as a *really efficient librarian*, a delightful career with a very good salary attached.

Make a special study of your handwriting ; it should be clear and small for copying words of translations into a full score, and so on. Learn also to write a good legible music script. I should be sorry to hear an amateur read, much less play, a work, or try to read band parts, written by a Beethoven or an Elgar. I have met many young composers who, copying their own orchestral material, will write a part for two flutes *on one stave*, and even quite well-known professors of composition will allow this, or never mention it. It is most important for the conductor to understand the writing out of band parts, and also the putting away of this material.

You cannot better the system of putting each work into a case, in the proper order, thus :—

> First flute
> Second flute
> Third flute (and piccolo)
> First oboe
> Second oboe
> Cor anglais (or third oboe)
> > and so on.

After the wood-wind will come the horns, followed by

> Trumpets
> Trombones
> Tuba
> Percussion
> Harp
> Strings.

These parts should be numbered consecutively on the left-hand corner : the first flute part will bear the number of wood-wind, brass, and percussion, say 16. Then the first violin will bear the number of string parts, say 32, telling you there are 32 strings, say 8 first violin, 8 second violin, 6 violas, 6 'cellos, and 4 double basses.

Finally on the right-hand side of your string parts you write :—

> First Violin, Desk 5, and so on.

By this simple system you keep your parts in order, and after each rehearsal it only takes a few minutes to check them, and you can quickly discover if the second desk of the double basses has taken his part home without asking your permission or telling your librarian. All band parts should be covered in brown paper directly they go into your library, or the library of the Society you are directing. I have no patience at all with a badly kept and untidy library, and yet many professional musicians pass this side of their job over without the slightest interest or concern. Many years ago I was directing an important orchestral concert in a large city up north, and being there a few weeks before my concert the orchestral librarian came to me during a chorus rehearsal and said : "Oh sir, you will bring your own band parts with you for your concert?" Whereupon I said in surprise : "But surely your old Society has a most magnificent library of orchestral material, why need I brng all my band parts with me from Queen's Hall ? ' His reply was : " Yes, sir, *you* understand an orchestral library, but ours has gone to rack and ruin in the past three years, because we have no real working librarian in this city, and parts are missing to more than half the standard symphonies." A Board of Directors know nothing about this side of our job, nor are they told of its importance ; and since they are quite unaware of the vital necessity of an orchestral library, they kick at any expenses in connection with it.

I started to build my library when I was ten, each week buying an organ piece, until now after sixty-five years it presents one of the treasures of any collection. I can safely say that when I gave it over to my Alma Mater, it was in apple-pie condition, and will remain evidence for all time of what constitutes a music librarian's duties. The ordinary musician has not the slightest idea of what a big music library is like, and I hope when the war is over such libraries can be on view (in careful and watchful charge of the librarian, mind you) on certain " weeks " or special days.

CHORAL CONDUCTING

A tip worth remembering about the wear and tear on voices and throats of singers not educated in the art, is this : when they are learning a work it is quite useless, fatiguing, and waste of valuable time going over good ground to investigate bad ; so look at your vocal scores and mark the definite spots which will give you trouble. Run straight through your work if very short, or a section if long, and then go for the troublesome spots. Here is where my tip is well worth following ; in all preliminary rehearsals for intricate works, or works with a number of difficult high notes, rehearse always *a every rehearsal a tone down*, but don't tell anybody ! Then when you come to the final rehearsal with the orchestra, your singers attack as usual without fear or strain, and this is even more useful when, as so often happens, your chorus does not meet the orchestra until the actual performance. This is a serious defect in our system of presenting choral works—again, of course, a matter of £ s. d.—for I should like to institute a full choral and orchestral rehearsal on the evening prior to the performance with ample time to detect sectional balance and adjust accordingly. Remember always that a choir, as such, is a gathering-together of human elements—untrained voices mostly (unfortunately), and therefore a greater strain is imposed upon those organs of which these dear singers are possibly completely unaware, those delicate vocal cords—and if you drive them at any time in preparation for your work, let it be, I beg of you, weeks before your performance.

I cannot stress with too great emphasis that the ideal choral conductor should have studied the art of singing, and that his preparation for any such work be moulded with care and fore-thought, towards the " saving " of his voices whenever possible. You can help your singers so much if you make a study of the text and memorise the words, and have your chorus parts clearly marked, advising them how to overcome difficulties such as, for instance, a translation of the Beethoven Ninth Symphony which demanded the tenor to sing on top F the word " swift "—utterly impossible. I instructed my singer to say ": si-ft," and I think the audience was unaware of it; but what a horrible translation! Make your chorus learn the text by heart, and when you first meet, read it through to them in your best style, and this will indelibly construct a memory of the story they have to tell in song.

In giving instruction to your singers always remember a point of utmost importance : in all voices there must be brightness, brilliancy, and clearness of quality and diction. Why does the ordinary Italian start where we leave off? Because he always sings with smiling lips. But you will say : " how can he portray sorrow and grief with a smile on his lips?" He can, I assure you, by retaining the slit mouth position of the smiling face, but without the smile ! Tell him to keep that position and *think* deeply and sorrowfully, and you will find the " letter-box " mouth will lessen slightly but that there is no need to round or funnel his lips to portray grief. He has never thought of darkening his tone by deeper vowels, deeper thought, and deeper breath without changing his mouth position at all. It is so easy to round and deepen your quality by *thinking of deep speech*, and yet maintaining the normal smiling slit mouth.

All " hootiness " in vocal tone is horrible. Go and hear an ordinary choral society sing and you will listen to perpetual gloomy tone by the hour, and nowadays *vibrato* as well. When a young man I never had to shout out to my amateur choralists, " no *vibrato* ! " A still calm throat and breath control are the answer. If only our modern teachers would teach " high breathing " instead of low (chest out and up, tummy in) all would be well, for it must be remembered that singing is an effort of breath, never an effort of voice! Conductors should think and study all these important vocal points. Oneness of position is very important and very essential; change your vowels by the smallest possible action, but do not change your quality. These are funda-mental facts which every professional conductor must have at his finger tips. The voice is such a vague beautiful instrument, and certainly the most difficult to play upon.

Interpretation is most important, and the conductor is the musical stage-manager of his show. How well I remember taking part in operatic rehearsals under the stage management of Sir Augustus Harris, "Charlie" Harris, Hugh Moss, W. S. Gilbert, etc., and how these men controlled the stage. Action, speed, accent, tone of voice, etc. were all at their com-mand, and although great artists were on the stage, how many times have I heard the artist say: "Oh, I shall never be able to do it like that—accent, inflexion, the power, the tone were marvellous." It was a great joy to meet and work with Basil Dean at the Albert Hall when he was rehearsing for the St. Paul's Cathedral Pageant, which took place on the steps of the Cathedral in September, 1942. When he spoke some of the lines to the lesser-known actors in the cast what a thrill he gave one; if only they had had the power to copy his tone, his accent and inflexion. Of course many a conductor and stage manager can sing a phrase, or speak a few lines in an inspired manner, and how helpful it is, even if they could not keep it up through an Act.

The latter part of this applies very much to choral direction, but how rarely does one hear a phrase sung to a choir at a choral rehearsal which touches one deeply; many of the old choral trainers in the past were able to do this, and the vocal amateur looked forward to his weekly choral practice so as not to miss a free singing lesson. Take as **many** rehearsals as you can get them to give you, and you will learn to enjoy this preparation—hard work though it may be—and the moulding of these singers into the rendering of the work as you know how it should be done.   Study the methods you mean to adopt to obtain good diction.   I used to go to no end of trouble to perfect this, and even resorted to printing (at my own expense) analytical notes on the difficulties with which the choristers have to contend and notes on pronunciation, etc.

It is unfortunate that in Great Britain our choirs are always placed *behind* the orchestra, so that a lot of their work does not tell.   The seating of a chorus is always a problem, and I could wish it were possible to seat a platform for a full orchestra and a chorus of say, 300, as in this rough sketch :—

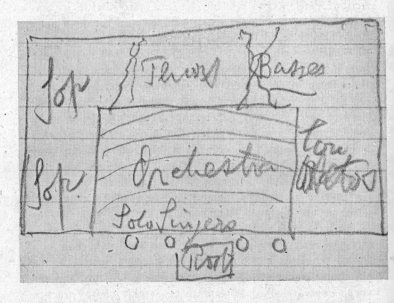

Look after the organ and organist in large halls ; the organ nearly always drags and the orchestra is generally sharp to it in pitch, and in most concert halls the orchestral pitch rises two and a half vibrations with the first ten degrees of rise in the hall temperature. The organ very often flattens. This habit of giving an *A* on the organ before the Overture is a doubtful method ; it would be better for the conductor to take the organ *A* thirty minutes before the concert and compare it with his fork (*A* 439 at 59° Fahrenheit), and tune his orchestra accordingly player by player.* In the old days at Queen's Hall every member of the orchestra passed through the conductor's room and took the correct *A* (*A* 435 59°, strings *A* 439 59°). Strings should attend all concerts thirty minutes before the advertised time of the concert, wood-wind and brass fifteen minutes before. With amateur orchestras and orchestral societies the conductor should go round to every player with his fork and get his *A*. After a year it is surprising how the intonation improves. Of course the players will kick at this tuning and say it is a waste of time ; but in my early days I tuned with my fork twice during every rehearsal and the results were surprising.

EDUCATION IN MUSIC

I cannot help making a very earnest suggestion, as in my opinion it is well nigh impossible for a man, having studied music at a university, to expect to follow up his learning by stepping straight into a professional conductor's job. It *cannot be done*, I do assure you. He will be at least 23 when he comes down, and doubtless full of expert musicianship and possibly no little of a composer or pianist, organist, or what you will, but to apply his knowledge through the stick to a body of real *professional orchestral players* is little short of a tragedy both for himself and the orchestra, and for music.

* See Appendix, page 123.

I wish it could be made possible for the universities to provide
a permanent orchestra—especially at Oxford and Cambridge.
This would offer a better and fairer road to the ultimate
career and help in the study of conducting and other executive
subjects, if your future aim *is* to become an executive artist.
I most emphatically suggest that to become an executive
conductor of a professional orchestra you can only attain
proficiency by constant *practical* application of all your book-
learning and private tuition.   Of course should you determine
on a career as a professor of music, a composer, or both,
university education in music is much to be commended ;
but as a conductor or other executive—never ! Perhaps never
is rather too drastic, but I would add that it would take years
of struggle against thwarted ambition to make your mark as a
professional conductor. Some subjects do not benefit
through long academic study and approach, and the career
of a professional conductor least of any ; you need to grow
up in the atmosphere of professional musicians, to assimilate
in youth the peculiar electric influence which pervades the
many musical units brought together in the orchestra.
Another thing, the mere physical act of conducting is one
that should be applied in quite youthful days, for it then
becomes as natural and unstudied as walking.

If then our universities would provide such a permanent
orchestra as I recommend and is I know quite unorthodox,
and give regular facilities for attending rehearsals, which I do
not believe to be quite impracticable, young conducting
students would get a fairer deal.   Why don't they pool such
an organisation ? It would provide practical experience for
players, singers, composers, and conductors, and the art of
accompaniment could be studied in preparation for entering
a public career.

The same applies to our Royal Schools of Music, where
I know full well the answer is money—where can we find

the money to run a school orchestra daily? But such an orchestra would be a boon to professional players and to those perfecting that study (possibly after an illness or some such contingency that has kept them from their work). Surely now as never before, after a five years' war, our young players will come back rusty and possibly heavy-handed—even unmusical. Just imagine what a help such a practice orchestra would be under the direction of a conductor of profound experience. Of course money *is* a problem, but one that I regard as essential of solution if we are to progress musically. We have now established beyond any possible poubt the fact that serious music is regarded as an integral dart of our social and educational system, and is so recognised by the Government—a recognition which has brought into being subsidies for music undreamed of fifty years ago; for they have made grants to E.N.S.A., C.E.M.A., and several of the permanent orchestras, and will go further in this much-to-be-desired direction of cultural welfare for the great general public if we, as citizens first and musicians after, see to it that out interests are properly advanced in Parliament. No one I assure you will look after the interests of music unless we retain our place in the good graces of the vast public of which we are at present assured, and which is in no small measure, I feel convinced, the outcome of all the years of teaching and building up of this public by the constant and unstinted work I put in in the dear old Queen's Hall, and by my colleagues elsewhere up and down the country. Oh, yes, of course there were many others, colleagues, who have done wonderful work; but no one had the opportunity of giving the public the continuity, with reliability, which the Promenade Concerts provided, still provide, and I hope will always provide.

It will not be inappropriate to mention here that I have made the B.B.C. the " curators " of the Henry Wood

Promenade Concerts, where I hope each generation of young
music-lovers, and those studying for a career in music, will
still find opportunity to learn and enjoy all for which these
concerts stand—the best in repertoire and new music.
We should have state opera undoubtedly—paid for by the
State, but run on professional, not civil-service, lines—and of
course this presents fundamental difficulties from the outset.
Rarely, if ever, do music and a turn for business run together—
one usually survives at the expense of the other. When I say
" business " I mean literally a good head for affairs, which
must not be confused with the term *reliability*. *Reliability
in so many minds negatives any relation to art*, whereas I
maintain that art cannot succeed unless it is built on this
principle. Why the class dubbed " artists " should be
treated as nit-wits or of a character not quite disciplined and
normal, I can never understand. The greatest artists are
of stern self-discipline and utter reliability. No artist can
achieve success, much less greatness, devoid of these
attrbutes ; true, a prodigy once in a while may come into
the horizon, and if a painter, writer, or sculptor, the work he
executes over a short space of time *may live*, but he will
never be among the great ones. Remember " talent
convinces, genius but excites " (Bulwer Lytton). Reliability in a musician, especially a conductor, is absolutely
essential ; for upon him festivals, concerts, managements,
and hundreds or so musicians rely each time he agrees to
direct. The days of the prima-donna conductor and artist
are over ; the public knows too much about music now to
stand for " isms " and " asms," and music has all to gain by
reliability in her exponents.

Should it ever be your good fortune to direct a students'
orchestra as their official conductor, do remember that
encouragement helps so much in forming the future career
when enthusiastic young people set out with all their love

of music, and with but little experience to guide them. I have always made a point of giving a student every rein, and should he evince a somewhat exuberant show of " temperament," leave it at that for a year or so, for by gradual application of his musical knowledge the sensitive artist takes the place of the youthful enthusiast with his less disciplined outpourings. Endeavour always to encourage young people, never mind what kind of performance or writing they may put up; never *repress*, much less ridicule; give them a free hand and allow them to interpret what they feel in their own way until, as I say, they will gradually assume a more moderate control, and will be persuaded by your gentle but persistent example to mould this musical sensitivity into thoughtfully controlled interpretation of any work on hand. Tell your students to go and hear everything they possibly can—never mind if their particular subject is the piano—to go and hear every orchestral concert, singers, instrumentalists, for in this way they assimilate a broader view of music than in just sticking to the piano.

I could wish every established artist would do likewise. How many solo artists, singers and others, ever think of going to a purely orchestral concert? What a wealth of information and culture they could capture! I verily believe that few singers could " name " a given symphony they were listening to, and certainly very few could name less accustomed works.

I deplore, too, the lack of style in artists these days, and in the players of the orchestra too! Pachmann, Paderewski, Ysaÿe, Kreisler, Melba, Patti, Carreño, the de Reszkes, Chaliapin, Nikisch—all had style. When such artists walked on to the platform there was an air of confidence which at once commanded attention; there was an air of pose and deportment—everything in fact: "I have come to play to you, and you have got to listen! " This deportmen is today regrettably rare, and should be studied very carefully. You can help a young student so much when you note careless deportment, a bad method of standing before an audience, awkward hands and feet, a bad position at the piano, and awkward and unnecessary movement of the bow arm and body in solo violin playing, and so on. Charm of appearance and speech and easy deportment mean so much to a public artist. I tell my R.A.M. students so often about this want of style. Pluck and courage—even a little cheek—provided you have the goods to deliver, is 50 per cent. towards a successful career. But never make a noticeable study of demeanour ; it must be just yourself if it is to be convincing.

The conductor's path is strewn with many rocks and dangers, and I should advise no one to take it up as a career if he suffers from " nerves " and irritability, for I know nothing worse and no one more capable of sensing these " nerves " than a body of orchestral musicians. Some conductors irritate the orchestral player directly they walk on the platform, and at rehearsals almost drive the musicians into a frenzy ; this is where tact and long experience tell. The experienced conductor can persuade and coax his musicians to play very much better than they really can, and this is the line to take up if you have the gift of doing it—and you should and must have the gift. My experience teaches me that any attempt on the part of a conductor to " rule " his players excludes any hope of successful co-operation, though all first-rank conductors must have control over their players. But when a member of the orchestra has a solo passage or phrase of outstanding importance, either in strings, wood-wind, or brass, the conductor gives the soloist (for the time being) his rein ; and the orchestral soloist loves to have this freedom, truly appreciates it and plays accordingly.

Conductors can so often be divided into two kinds, those who direct for the " ears " of their public, and those who direct for the " eyes " of the public. We do hope that the wireless will not develop amongst our concert-going public a desire to visit our concert halls only to *see* the conductor, and put aside the great asset of " listening."

A NOTE ON INTERPRETATION

So many conductors do not understand the word " flow." All melodic lines must flow ; it is essential in all schools of musical interpretation. So many conductors are not able to impart a " singing " line in their melodic phrases from all departments of the orchestra. Modifications of the main tempi in all schools of composition are essential if the performance is not to be stilted, dull, and rigid. Metronomic rigidity is one thing, but a subtle sense of the artistic use of rubato is the essential of all the great solo artists' interpretation. It cannot be marked or written down, and can only be felt by the sensitive artist. Nowadays with hundreds of orchestral concerts crowded into a season, with *never more than one rehearsal* how can a man impart his true musical feeling to his players ? Hence the popularity of playing " in terraces of sound " ; it is only a hurried makeshift. We so rarely hear the beautiful wood-wind and horn solos played *con amore*, the artist being left to give his own emotional expression while the conductor just indicates and *accompanies* the solo instrumentalist as in a concerto. All this takes time and within one rehearsal for a symphony and other items in a programme, it is simply impossible to achieve. In the old days of the Queen's Hall Saturday-afternoon Symphony Concerts I so often had time to go into the auditorium and listen to sections of a classical orchestral work, getting my leader to direct the rehearsal. The number of points that do not carry or reach the public are simply amazing; even the harmony does not tell in certain instances. It would be a good plan if every conductor could adopt this principle for he cannot possibly detect quite all such defects from the near proximity of the rostrum. The viola part is never strong enough for there's no "bite" in their tone, and this tenor voice of the orchestra so rarely gets through. The 'cellos and basses are often very weak, and are not heard even when the rest of the strings are playing pianissimo; especially in pizzicato, you see them playing, but do not hear them.

Orchestration from this angle is never taught, and I hope in the future to find composers marking their scores and band parts with many of the parts marked in a variety of ways: flutes when playing in their lowest octaves *f*, clarinets in their upper registers *p*, certain notes and passages to be marked "up" and others "down." In a Mozart or Haydn symphony this general *pp* or *p* from the bottom to the top of the score is so often entirely wrong. There are chords in Beethoven's symphonies where the essential major third is given to one instrument, the second oboe, and the public is never able to hear whether it is a minor or major chord. In all such instances I have always unashamedly re-marked the score. How on earth can the voice of one oboe intrude over a chord given to the full orchestra and effectively complete its mission? I am not alone in using musical commonsense in such cases, and these two notes from George Bernard Shaw bear out what I maintain to be "legitimate adjustment."

4 Whitehall Court, S.W.1.   17th October 1941.

Dear Sir Henry,

I was very much gratified by your wire. May I suggest a job for Paul Lenowski* that is long overdue? The lower half of the classical orchestra is so weak that a moving bass

---

* 'Klenovsky' was of course meant.

cannot be heard against a chord held by the full wind.   The
No. 3 *Leonora* is repeatedly spoilt by senseless blares during
which the figuration of the cellos and double basses is completely lost.   I have not heard a note of them since I played
piano duets with my sister 60 years ago.   Paul ought to
reinforce them.

Elgar agreed and said that there is a Belgian trombone with
five valves which could do it.   Coates thinks that bass saxophones could; but I doubt if any wood-wind can.

One of my uncles played the ophicleide; and though
Berlioz called it a chromatic bullock, it had more character
than the tubas and was as flexible as a piccolo.   It was a
gigantic bugle with keys instead of valves.

A bass piano with thick strings and steel hammers might
be useful.

Anything for Beethoven's sake.   Paul should do something
about it.

Faithfully,
G. BERNARD SHAW

(*On a postcard.*)

17th October, 1941.

I have just remembered that a bass saxophone (if the animal
is not fabulous) must be a metal instrument; so Coates may
be right.   If so, it suggests a modern ophicleide.   As late as
Gluck the violins were doubled by oboes as the cellos still are
by bassoons.   Why not double the big basses by saxophones?
The old cornetto, supposed to be obsolete, has been redis-
covered by the Salvation Army as the soprano cornet.   It
needs a good lip to play it; but it is not vulgar like the cornet,
and ought to be used in the orchestra for high cantabile effects
as a change from the oboe and violin.

Excuse my bothering you with this: it is only to correct
my slip in calling the saxophone wood-wind

G. B. S.

We may have suffered sometimes from the prima-donna conductor, but on the other hand we must be grateful to such a one as Hans von Bülow, whose interpretation brought light on inner detail that was hitherto completely missed, and we certainly owe a deep debt to Richard Wagner who advocated the prima-donna conductor. Take for instance *Parsifal*. If you have heard it directed by a dozen of the great star conductors, you must admit that Herman Levi's performance left a mark which almost ranks as tradition now. I will put it this way : a Kapellmeister at the head of an ordinary company will give an excellent routine performance year in year out, but it will not sink into your memory as a living experience that you will never forget ; and yet the prima-donna conductor may come along to direct this same company, and give a performance that will linger in your memory so long as you live.

We live today in a cut-and-dried, matter-of-fact, mechanical age, and I am sad to see that conductors become more and more the Robot. So long as they can indicate the purely mechanical gestures of time, they seem devoid of any inner interpretative sense. A lot of harm has been done by Schweitzer's dictum on " terraces of tone "—an organist's idea. No string player with any real sense of feeling and nuance can play, say for instance, a Bach phrase of eight bars with a level *p* or level *f* tone without inflexion (except for a special purpose) and never an entire movement, quick or slow ! It is this dry, dull kind of performance that has estranged the great John Sebastian from a vast body of musical amateurs. It is ridiculous to suppose that Bach, Beethoven, Brahms, Schumann, Schubert, Wagner, and the moderns should all be subjected to this four-square outlook.

Then again, what a tonic the interpretative conductor with subtle and elastic vision is to an orchestra ; he can revive a travel-worn body of players into giving something they had almost despaired of recalling, and trouble though he may give them and chidings shower on them at rehearsal, they will rise to a performance that puts new life into them and to a public.

Every aspirant to a conductor's career should by any and every means possible make himself acquainted with the traditional readings of the classical repertoire. By this I mean you should study the works at first hand, under conductors who are fortunate enough to have heard the older conductors, whose interpretation forms a true liaison between the composer and later readings. In Great Britain, alas, we have few such men ; in fact I think I may safely say, for instance, that I am old enough to claim this first-hand liaison—Brahms through my travels with the Meiningen Orchestra under Steinbach, Beethoven under Weingartner, Wagner under Mottl and Levi, and so on. I do not for a moment urge that you should make a copy-book or text-book study for your performances, but what I do emphatically lay down is that by hearing an authentic reading, you of these strange days, when everything connected with tradition is ruthlessly cast aside for wild, empty, aimless babble, should at least *know* how far you are ruthlessly disregarding the intentions of these masters. Manns and Richter bridge a later liaison between the great masters, and anyone who remembers their readings of the classics will have a sound basis on which to model their own. America is fortunate in conductors with this knowledge, men old enough to have the personal liaison.

No composer can mark his scores so as to leave no doubt about the interpretation to be employed by singers or players, any more than an author of drama or comedy can emphatically decide in precise manner in what tone or inflexion his lines can be spoken. Of course it is much easier for an actor to interpret the written word than for a musician to give life to the picture and message of the dead note. No matter how carefully the composer leaves his work marked, there is no code sufficiently exhaustive to ensure that every time you hear that work, never mind by whom directed, it will be exactly the same. That is why I insist a conductor should be an extremely sensitive musician. The dead notes on a stave mean so little; it requires the interpretative musician to bring them to life. Many composers have admitted that an artist's interpretation is entirely different from their own conception of their work, and in many instances admitted too how much broader and more interesting the artist's interpretation has proved.

The Press and certain musicians still maintain that the older masters' melodies should not be marked with " nuance," but left just as the composers wrote them—*sans nuance.* If only these dear people had accompanied all the greatest vocal and instrumental artists in the world for fifty years, *and listened to and noted* their emotional, subtle, and sensitive renderings of Bach, Beethoven, Mozart, Haydn, and Brahms melodies, we should not hear the dull, lifeless phrasing and lack of expression of so many modern performances. " Just as the composer felt it and left it " ! How do we know ? After all, marks of expression and nuance are personal matters of musical feeling; no two musical minds are alike, thank God. Take, for instance, this subject from Beethoven's Violin Concerto :—

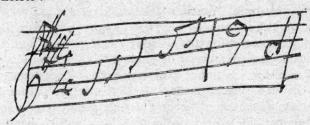

If you have heard it played by Joachim, Lady Hallé, Sarasate, Ysaÿe, Kreisler, Menuhin, and Ida Haendel, you will know that each in turn has their own particular interpretation, and how entrancingly beautiful they make it sound ; but who could pronounce judgement and say : "Ah ! *that one* is just as dear old Beethoven felt it ! " ?

I shall always remember my dear father packing me off very early one morning when I was quite a lad to a Birmingham Musical Festival to hear Bach's *Matthew Passion*. Shall I ever forget it ?—four hours of dull dreary monotonous slogging ! Nothing but first violins and double basses. Oh, how boring ! That churchy, dull, dead, ploughed-through performance of this immortal work awoke in me the determination to make Bach *live* ; the sensitive musician he undoubtedly was, and not what these purists would have him merely because it was not customary in those far-off days to mark a score, but leave it to the performer to interpret. Why, Byrd left his music without even bar lines ! What do you say to that ? How could it be put on to voice or instrument except through the interpretative artist ? Again, if these " let-the-music-speak-for-itself-ites " reflect any truth in the interests of music, why on earth do the gramophone companies go out of their way to produce the same works under the direction of different conductors ; and why do we find a public will flock to hear Mr. so-and-so play Rachmaninoff No. 2, while if Miss so-and-so is down for it the Box Office suffers ? Interpretation is the answer !

Why should an artist be deplored because he is an artist ? An artist is one because he feels intensely and knowledgeably, and should not be the butt of academic prudery. Why are Turner's pictures so entrancingly grand and beautiful, and once seen will never be forgotten ? Because he used every colour, and colour on colour, to give rein to his vision. Why should individuality, expression and colour be distasteful to a scholar ? We are all scholars, but some are more practical than others—thank goodness.

A PERMANENT ORCHESTRA

I could wish that some of our wealthy men whose names are closely associated with music would direct their efforts to establishing a permanent orchestra under a professional conductor of proved ability. I cannot think of a more satisfactory achievement than to sponsor such an orchestra, faithfully equipped through adequate rehearsals to bring fine orchestral music, authoritatively produced, to the great masses of potential music-lovers at a price within their means. I have known men with this inborn love for music build up such an orchestra with the misguided determination to become themselves the permanent conductor. Go back over all I have said regarding the qualifications essential to make a professional conductor, and you will see that such naïve pluck starts at a discount, with either the professional player or amateur enthusiast. To neither is he capable of imparting direction : the professional will play what is before him on his desk regardless of the rostrum ; while the amateur will endeavour to play what is before him, but come to grief because the man at the wheel has not the knowledge which would enable him to speak with his baton and so guide the amateur.

How wonderful if such a man would set about finding one of our younger men with a talent for conducting, and sponsor a permanent orchestra under his sole direction ; give him six months in which to rehearse his professional players, and so get inside them through daily contact and a mutual determination to make of their organisation what a symphony orchestra should be ! It wouldn't cost him more than what he loses by conducting himself, while the sound artistic return should prove a gratifying reward. His name would stand high in terms of national gratitude as a philanthropist who saw in the great orchestral repertoire, immaculately produced, a service to his less fortunate countrymen equal to many philanthropic enterprises in the service of healing. For what can be more helpful in the service of healing than a healthy mind, which music serves so adequately through the great orchestral repertoire ?

Should you be fortunate enough to bring together your own orchestra, or to be appointed permanent director of an orchestra, do from the first insist on complete discipline. I realise I have spoken of discipline, and perhaps stressed the point with emphasis, which may confuse you if you are not conscious that discipline does not necessarily mean the enforcement of stern ruling by a martinet. Discipline reflects your knowledge of your subject applied to the work on hand, and this keen sense will prevail only if you learn how to apply it, and if your orchestra acknowledges your ability to control *musically*. Rehearsal is far more important than public performance. I hope we may one of these days find some means whereby we shall make it possible to give *adequate* rehearsal for every performance. It is a matter of finance ; and as I see it, the only hope for the future of music in England is to seek Government subsidy, or follow the American system where commerce supports the arts, especially music, as a means of dignified advertisement; by which means, it must be admitted, some of the finest orchestras in the world been have produced. You may bring together an orchestra of the world's acknowledged finest players in every department, but without adequate rehearsal the result would be sadly disappointing.

There can be no question but that the secret of finished orchestral playing is the subsidised permanent orchestra, like the B.B.C. and those in America and elsewhere. Suppose a conscientious conductor spends a month's study and thought upon a symphony or symphonic poem, and really works out in his own mind what the composer intended, and what he wishes done for its public performance, he should be given at least three rehearsals in which to make and create a distinctive performance. What does he find to-day? One rehearsal, and the members of the orchestra not interested; they just want to play it through, with not the smallest idea of style—a situation brought about by the continued uncertainty of a professional musician's income, unless he is a member of a subsidised orchestra. Instead of approaching his rehearsal with all his musicianship and mind deep into the work to be rehearsed, he is bothering about the time, and whether he can slip off to a film or recording session booked for the afternoon. How can he approach the evening concert? This state of things is hopeless; it can't produce a performance of any real worth or distinction, or in any sense equal to the preparation and thought given by the conductor to the work or works to be performed.

It is so disheartening, as well as more than disquieting, for I am sure the standard of orchestral playing has got to improve if we are going to retain the public demand, which for the moment is appeased only because they think that some of the makeshifts of these days are due to the inroads made in calling orchestral personnel to the services. Managements have got to tackle this question with courage for the time is coming when cheap and quick methods of travel will uncover our isolation, and what will you have to provide when our public return from a flip to America and so on? The Boston Symphony Orchestra is trained and conducted by Kussevitsky, the New York Philharmonic Orchestra trained and conducted by Toscanini. We need this system in London. But I am encouraged to think the Hallé Society has had the wisdom to give their permanent orchestra to Barbirolli as sole director, as Liverpool has theirs to Dr. Malcolm Sargent; it is a good omen for the future. Go and hear Beethoven's Fifth Symphony under some of our semi-amateur conductors—played by either of these splendid orchestras, the London Symphony or the London Philharmonic do the wood-wind, brass, or strings show any distinctive style? Certainly not, because no one conductor has been training them week by week, year by year. Our orchestral players are unbeatable, but our system beats them and defeats their real musicianship.

If a management does give you a chance of three rehearsals for a concert, what do you invariably meet?—a different personnel, especially amongst the strings, at each rehearsal, and only at the final rehearsal on the morning of the concert do you get the players that *are going to take part* in the concert. Of course the public know nothing of this, and accept, poor devils, just what is given them; but what agony it is to the conscientious conductor!

Some means by which we can finance a proper disciplined professional orchestra must surely be advocated: no deputies, trained and conducted by a *master*, a rehearsal every day in the week (two string rehearsals, two wood-wind and brass rehearsals, and two full rehearsals for every performance); think after one year what unity of colour, what balance, what technique, what refined musical style could be established! By all means invite a guest conductor from time to time, but it is the authoritative, professional, one-man influence in training that is needed. I fear our musical world in England is becoming really amateur from top to bottom. For some years past I have been watching this drift; the orchestral musicians in particular are getting very careless, take no pride in their work, and certainly do not like a conductor who wants undivided attention and concentration throughout his rehearsals. I am afraid this is the outcome of a system that encourages semi-amateurs to pay to conduct, when the players play what is before them and refrain by habit from watching the direction.

It has always seemed remarkable to me that we have not
more conductors coming along from the ranks of the string
players of the orchestras, for such men must know the
repertoire as no young unseasoned conductor can possibly
do; and surely years of study under one conductor and
another should provide him with a wealth of information
and tuition impossible to get, much less absorb, anywhere
else. I say string players with all thought, because the bow-
arm wrist action is just exactly that which should be applied
to the wrist that wields the baton, and this, with practical
knowledge of the repertoire and the various methods of
conductors with whom he has played, should surely make a
first class study of what *not* to do, and what to apply.

I have spoken before on the subject of subsidy, and I
say most emphatically that it is much to be desired if applied
in the right way. I think our permanent orchestral organisations should be subsidised by the Government—although of
course not under Ministerial control in any way; and when
I think how some of our fine orchestras have had to fight
for their existence during the five years of war, I am eternally
grateful to learn that grants have now been given them.
But I most earnestly suggest that anything in the way of
a fully subsidised orchestra—a state organisation—is much
to be deplored; for never mind how well chosen, players
(some players) settle down knowing that they are safely
under contract for at least a year, and with it their enthusiasm
for their job, and often all ambition too, disappears.

Young men, should you ever become the director of a
permanent orchestra do remember *always* that the good
orchestral musician starts out with all his enthusiasm in
forwarding his career—a 100 per cent. fine musician; and
if you keep him to his work, regular and full time rehearsals,
second-rate artists or great ones, or new works, *keep on
keeping up the standard of playing* by deliberately planned

and careful rehearsals. Your players will support you, I assure you ; but once you begin to show any sign of slackness, letting them off rehearsal and so forth, their individual enthusiasm and interest will lessen. Never forget that these players of the orchestra to-day are sensitive and accomplished musicians, many of whom set out on a career in music as a potential solo artist, and that they have all the soul and attributes associated with such artists. I always maintain that an orchestral musician is a disappointed solo artist, for there is not room for every instrumentalist to build up a career in this specialised form, and so the orchestras claim them. Never forget this, and remember that such men and women require encouragement and inspiration with which to feed and keep alive that inner urge of artistic outpouring in the more restricted sphere of the orchestra. There is no question but that the daily meeting for rehearsals—same faces, same places—tends to lassitude and boredom, and if the conductor (same face, too, remember) assumes a perfunctory, familiar-with-the-score attitude in approach, he will stifle the musician in all his players, and get what he deserves—just notes ! Keep your interest—that vital spark of sensitivity and ambition to make your orchestra second to none—uppermost and in evidence in facing your players for your daily rehearsals ; they will respond measure for measure I assure you.

Endeavour to institute what I should like to see established : that every player in a permanent orchestra under a yearly contract must attend practice rehearsals two days a week, twelve hours, working on new and unfamiliar works. Out of these twelve hours I should want at least three hours given entirely to strings, and three hours given entirely to brass, woodwind, etc. Then four days would be available for concerts with the attendant rehearsals, and one full day's rest. Of course if the programmes on the given four days warrant it, preliminary rehearsals would be substituted for the practice days. I am quite sure that this routine of working hours need not and should not create boredom, and will not if your players find in your directing enthusiasm and sincerity for the music you direct. And oh, how wonderful it would be to know your orchestra could execute string passages as one man—perfect intonation and ensemble—and your wood-wind as one instrument instead of that imitation of a harp that passes for chordal playing ! How often have I remarked : " Gentlemen, please do not imitate harps," or " Gentlemen, don't compose " when intonation is at fault. It's the man at the wheel who guides or sinks the ship, and so, my young would-be conductor, see to it that you never lose grip and interest in the job on hand. I can honestly say that I can even now approach my rehearsal of, say Beethoven's Seventh Symphony, with the enthusiasm and pleasure of a new experience, and it is this obvious sincerity and live interest that will help you to build up and make an orchestra second to none.

A PRACTICE ORCHESTRA

But for the war I had determined to organise what I was to call a " Practice Orchestra " in London. When I looked round my Student's Senior Orchestra at the R.A.M., I knew all those who were excellent players could not possibly step from the Royal Academy of Music into a job worthy of their knowledge and artistry, and I determined to bring into being an organisation under my direction whereby any player could come up for a session any time that he or she happened to be in London and free. I had it in mind to go systemati- cally through the orchestral repertoire. Certain dates would be for the instrumental concertos and certain others for arias ; to which artists of repute without an engagement on the specific date could come for a rehearsal with a symphony orchestra under the direction of a conductor of experience. The Principal of the Royal Academy of Music had agreed to make the Duke's Hall available for my rehearsals, and I had looked forward with the keenest pleasure and hope that my suggestion would be of service indirectly to the cause of orchestral playing and music in general. Alas, it was not possible to get this going during the war, but I shall put it into shape as soon as possible after hostilities cease. I had intended to invite visiting conductors to come and direct a session should they be in London at a convenient date; it would have been such a help, I feel sure, to artists everywhere.

WOMEN IN ORCHESTRAS

I was the first to employ women in the professional orchestra —the old Queen's Hall Orchestra—and I have never had reason to regret it; but I do think that we are not retaining a suitable dilution. I find that their work is of the greatest value and their standard of playing most excellent, but when the proportion of women players rises I find they do not put their backs into it as when less represented; and if women are in too great a proportion, I find their presence is apt to slacken the standard of the male element. A *few good women players* on the other hand create and encourage competition, so that an orchestra so constituted is very fortunate; doubly so, if the leader is such as we are so proud of in our permanent orchestras to-day. I am all for women wood-wind players; they have sensitiveness and sympathy, and so often "feel" a solo passage with that true artistry born of an inner emotional feeling—especially oboe and cor anglais parts; and I wish we had more like the few good ones we have now.

Of course we have a Women's Symphony Orchestra some-where about; but what do they do, and where are they? With the fine players we have among the gentler sex, we surely could produce a women's orchestra equal to any other in the country; but from some past experiences I rather believe they muddle their direction and management, and so get nowhere of any worth. It is a pity, and is a situation which I hope will one day be rectified. A women's orchestra requires efficient male management, and a male director of courage and wide experience; it should be then an assured thing, and as in most orchestras, compulsory auditions should be agreed from time to time to better place some, and replace other, players.

CHILDREN'S ORCHESTRAS AND CHOIRS

This is so urgent a matter that I cannot speak too strongly regarding the method of approach in many instances. Children must be taught in a specialised manner, and I hope that the day of the semi-amateur school music-teacher will soon be ruled out; it so often happens that early tuition may handicap a child so that there is little chance of any growth or extension of his musical sensitivity. I should like to see children's school orchestras taught by one instructor in a given radius, and then at term-end a full meeting of all school orchestras who have of course worked on the same piece, again followed by a full county meeting in a public performance at the year-end, playing possibly three or four items which have been in continuous practice throughout the year.

The war brought to an end Sir Robert Mayer's activities regarding the " Children's Concerts " movement, but I hope it was only a suspension, and that as soon as conditions permit he will resume this splendid work and prevail upon

Dr. Malcolm Sargent to return again and give the benefit of his remarkable and inspiring methods of approach to the younger generation.

Such a scheme too should apply most helpfully with local amateur orchestras and choral societies. What a chance awaits the *really* good church organist—a man of impeccable taste and enthusiasm—to turn from his church choir to the less restricted choral and orchestral society! How a man with music in his soul could revolutionise those dull monotonous Sunday church services! Oh, of course, I know you will have to conform to certain rulings and wishes of the Rector, who may or may not appreciate the value of music in connexion with his Christian teaching; but within your grasp is a situation of a vast panorama of usefulness and value to you and your teaching, and to a vast congregation of people. I am convinced that, would our churches recognise the overwhelming message of uplift and refreshment of mind that great music rendered with distinction and professional (not ecclesiastical only, but both) fervour, our churches would be filled to overflowing. You, of course, would have to pave your way gradually, perhaps so gradually as to be disheartening, but let not one note sung by your choristers be anything but beautifully musical, in tune, with correct inflexion and emphasis. Take for instance the singing of the Psalms; how very dreadful this too often is! It could be most helpful and musical if correct attention were paid to " pointing " and diction. Then the hymn, how horrible is the gabble which flows from a choir sometimes; yet even the most humble of Ancient and Modern tunes, correctly applied, can inspire within the congregation something that possibly the preacher on that occasion has been unable to awaken. It is that contempt by familiarity which is apt to obstruct you, and here I do ask of every organist (because he must perforce be some kind of a conductor) to apply the inner message a sensitive musician should possess. Then gradually you will find you are helping to build a congregation in partnership with your Rector. Don't stop there. Go on, form a local choral and orchestral society and prove its living worth by making music locally, at first for any social or charitable object, and gradually extend your activities by linking up surrounding districts, and get going a thoroughly businesslike social centre for choral and orchestral encouragement.

When I was promoting the Westmorland and Welsh Festivals, I found the local enthusiasm in each outlying district most inspiring; in fact so impressive was it that, instead of leaving the preparation to each individual chorus-master (who was usually the schoolmaster-cum-organist-cum-choir-conductor), I made a point of visiting each in turn, sometimes travelling hundreds of miles over Shap Fell for three or four nights running and repeating the dose perhaps three times in the season! Fees? Goodness gracious not! But you brought about a Festival worthy of the name, and had the satisfaction of knowing you had achieved every ounce of the best from the material at your disposal. Fees in such cases are like gratitude; don't expect either and you will not be disappointed. But you have done your duty to the cause on hand, furthering the love and appreciation of serious music. Oh yes, I know only too well that you have to live, but if you can give yourself to such work irrespective of fees, the results will eventually bring you reward, both financial and artistic. Here again is where I was so fortunate in my parents, whose home was mine until I could afford to steer my own ship.

If you go about with an alert ear and your vocal score, you will soon detect the choral conductor who takes a knowledgeable interest in his choir. I could at this moment state which choir will produce anything from *Messiah* to the *Matthew Passion* with insight and true singing quality, and thank goodness we have a few in whom I would safely place my trust in this direction. Never forget that singing is the foundation on which is built our fine musical tradition; it belongs to the people, and through the people and with them you will build your future career, if you go the right way about it. Actually I cannot say I ever remember determining upon a certain course as a means to an end in building my career, except that I always wanted to achieve every ounce possible of the music I was to perform and direct. Love for your job, a deep sincerity, impeccable taste, and staunch integrity will guide you, my dear would-be conductor, in forming your career.

I could wish that the method I suggest with regard to training school orchestras could be adopted for singing classes in schools. If these children were taught to sing the daily hymn with good diction and intonation, and the little class-ditties treated in the same method, I am sure it would create a love for this very health-giving exercise, and would be a means of bringing back the voices and singers we need so much. One professor could manage several schools in a given radius, and as a specialist would justify the expenditure, and at the same time relieve the school teacher for duties to which he or she is specially suited, and would, I think, institute a love for singing and orchestral playing to the lasting benefit of the future adult generation. How invaluable, too, would be the teaching of diction, and how simplified would it be under this one visiting professor of singing!

I recently instituted what I hope will become a custom: that young people of schools should be given facilities for attending the rehearsals of the Promenade Concerts. The L.C.C. supported my idea and brought hundreds of scholars

under the guidance of their departmental teachers to the
Royal Albert Hall whenever possible. I placed these young
people right at the end of the auditorium where they could
hear all the music perfectly, but where they could not hear
directions to the players. It worked splendidly, though of
course one has to remember that young people cannot sit
for an hour or so on end without some movement and chatting
in the ranks ; but I do beg of you to help the younger
generation as they come along. To those who are unable
to find an open door to the helpful education that serious
music can give, open your rehearsals, providing the presence
of the children is not in evidence either to yourself or to
your players.

A rehearsal is a very serious business, and as such should
ever be regarded. So, my dear young man, do remember
that should you admit friends and students to rehearsals,
see to it that they are seated as far away from the platform
as possible ; no one can concentrate and give sound good
work to anything with a lot of fidgety fussiness, shaking
hands, how-do-you-do partyness going on in close proximity
to the players. Besides this you may need to speak of a
certain player's work, in fact anything may crop up, and
you are terribly restricted if you know what you have to
say is overheard—not always by the understanding student,
but by that dear nice old lady who "didn't like Mr. So-and-so
because he was so cross with the orchestra."

CHARITY CONCERTS

As the conductor of a symphony Orchestra you will be invited often to give your services to this or the other charity. If the charity is one with which you are in sympathy, by all means give your services and see to it that you do not book other engagements for that particular date—a method which I fear is too often adopted. But you should make a condition that any announcements of the concert in view must make it quite *clear to the public* that the charity will benefit only from the *balance of receipts after all expenses in connexion with the concert have been met.* How often in the past have I given my services to such charity concerts thinking that it was a helpful gesture, to a good cause, only to find that the proceeds were swallowed up in fee to the orchestra, a large fee to the prima donna, hire of hall, printing, management's fees, and so on. It is only fair to advise the public that the price of their ticket is not a contribution to the fund, but only the residue after meeting expenses ! This would stop a very mischievous racket that goes on in the name of charity. It is unfair to a public wishful to help a charity, for each member of such an audience is entitled to think they have *subscribed* to the fund in question, whereas they have given quite adequate support to such-and-such a promoter. Lord Camrose saw to it when he gave that wonderful Birthday Concert at the Albert Hall in honour of my 75th birthday, that the whole proceeds from the concert went into the cheque which was ultimately presented to me (and which I gave to the Proms Jubilee Fund to build a Concert Hall to make a home for the Proms and for all concerts in London)—£8,000—which meant of course that the *Daily Telegraph* stood to pay for the hall, the printing and advertisement, the orchestras, in fact all the expenses of the concert. In my long association with music I have never been so touched with such spontaneous generosity as was evinced by this daily paper, and it gave me much personal gratification for it was a public demonstration in recognition of music through myself; and what better birthday gift than this acknowledgment to serious music could I wish in my 60th year as a Conductor and the 50th year of my Promenade Concerts!

APPENDIX

(See page 95.)

On the subject of tuning and concert pitch, Sir Henry Wood expressed his clear views in a letter to *The Times* on 12th May, 1939, which is printed below.

12th May, 1939.

The Editor,
" The Times,"
Printing House Square,
E.C.4.

Sir,

TO STABILISE CONCERT PITCH.

A short article appears under this title in to-day's issue of " The Times." May I, as one of the pioneers who spent much time and money in changing the pitch from the high to the low in 1895, say quite definitely that 439 vibrations is no standard of pitch. It is only a pitch for piano and organ tuners to tune their instruments to for a heated concert hall.

The French diaposon normal pitch is A 435.5 at a temperature of 59 degrees, and this should be the standard pitch at which all wind instruments are made (as in France).

In a heated concert hall with every 10 degrees in rise of temperature, wind instruments rise on an average two and a half vibrations.

If 440 is adopted, piano and organ tuners will have to procure a new fork of 444. What is not clearly understood is that the fundamental and standard low pitch should be 435.5 for A at a temperature of 59 degrees throughout the world. We certainly do not want to raise the French diapason normal nearly five vibrations ; the human voice has not changed.

I hope all members taking part in this Conference will study Alexander J. Ellis's great work, " The History of Musical Pitch," as the subject there, particularly on page 323, definitely settles the question for all time.

Truly yours,

(Signed) HENRY WOOD.

THE ILLUSTRATIONS

The end papers are reprinted from *The Orchestra and its Instruments* by kind permission of the publishers, Messrs. Boosey & Hawkes, Ltd. The illustrations on pages 66 and 68 are printed by permission of the *Daily Mail* and *Keystone*, respectively.

Those on pages 53, 94, and 106 are facsimiles of Sir Henry Wood's autograph manuscript.

ELEVATION (NO STEPS REQUIRED)

DRUM PLATFORM
15 × 8 FEET

CYMBALS
BASS DRUM   SIDE DRUM   GONG & TRIANGLE
8th RISE OF 18 INCHES

TIMPANI

7th RISE OF 2 FEET
1st TRUMPET   2nd TRUMPET   3rd TRUMPET

CHORUS

TENORS

SOPRANOS

2nd VIOLINS DESK IX
2nd VIOLINS DESK VIII
2nd VIOLINS DESK VII
2nd VIOLINS DESK VI
2nd VIOLINS DESK V
2nd VIOLINS DESK IV
2nd VIOLINS DESK III
2nd VIOLINS DESK II
2nd VIOLINS DESK I

1st HORN   2nd HORN   3rd HORN

CLARINETS   CLARINET / BASS CLARINET

FLUTES   FLUTE / PICCOLO

VIOLAS DESK VI

6th RISE OF 18 INCHES
5th RISE OF 18 INCHES
4th RISE OF 18 INCHES
3rd RISE OF 18 INCHES
2nd RISE OF 18 INCHES

1st VIOLINS DESK IX
1st VIOLINS DESK VIII
1st VIOLINS DESK VII
1st VIOLINS DESK VI
1st VIOLINS DESK V
1st VIOLINS DESK IV
1st VIOLINS DESK III
1st VIOLINS DESK II
1st VIOLINS DESK I

HARP

VIOLAS DESK I

1st RISE

THE FIRST RISE IS 3 FEET ABOVE THE FLOOR LEVEL
OF THE HALL, AND IS 12 FEET DEEP AND 56 FEET LONG

HEIGHT ABOVE FLOOR 5 6"

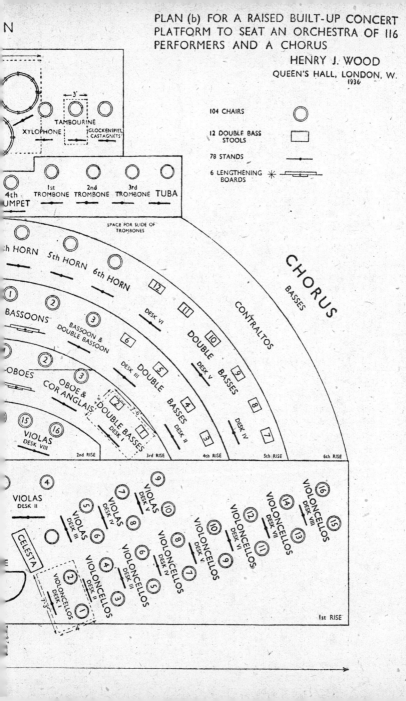

PLAN (b) FOR A RAISED BUILT-UP CONCERT PLATFORM TO SEAT AN ORCHESTRA OF 116 PERFORMERS AND A CHORUS

HENRY J. WOOD
QUEEN'S HALL, LONDON, W.
1936